PARENTS, PROFESSIONALS AND MENTALLY
HANDICAPPED PEOPLE

Parents, Professionals and Mentally Handicapped People

APPROACHES TO PARTNERSHIP

Edited by
PETER MITTLER and HELEN McCONACHIE

BROOKLINE BOOKS
29 Ware Street
Cambridge, MA 02138
(617) 868-0360

Library of Congress Cataloging in Publication Data
Main entry under title:

Parents, professionals and mentally handicapped people.

Papers from a seminar held at the University of
Manchester, 1981, which was sponsored by the Bishop
Bekkers Foundation, Utrecht, and jointly organised
by the Bishop Bekkers Institute and the Hester Adrian
Research Centre, in association with the International
League of Societies for Persons with Mental Handicap.
    Bibliography: p.
    Includes index.
    1. Mentally handicapped – Family relationships –
Congresses. 2. Mentally handicapped – Europe – Family
relationships – Congresses. 3. Mentally handicapped –
Services for – Europe – Congresses. I. Mittler, Peter J.
II. McConachie, Helen. III. Bishop Bekkers Institute.
IV. Hester Adrian Research Centre. V. International
League of Societies for Persons with Mental Handicap.
HV3004.P37   1984   362.3'8   84-23751
ISBN 0-914797-12-3

Printed and bound in Great Britain

CONTENTS

SECTION FOUR: THE SCHOOL YEARS

SECTION FIVE: ADOLESCENCE AND ADULTHOOD

SECTION SIX: DISCUSSION AND FOLLOW-UP

TABLES AND FIGURES

This book is affectionately dedicated to Dorothy Jeffree on the occasion of her retirement from the Hester Adrian Research Centre, in recognition of her outstanding work in promoting partnership between parents, professionals and mentally handicapped people.

ACKNOWLEDGEMENTS

The editors wish to thank Beryl Sweeney and Norma Bewley for their careful typing. We are very grateful to the National Council for Special Education for permission to adapt Chapter 1 of this volume from the pamphlet *Partnership with Parents* (Peter Mittler and Helle Mittler, 1982) in the series 'Developing Horizons in Special Education', and also to Ballière Tindall (Publishers) for permission to reproduce Figure 5.1 from *Tredgold's Mental Retardation, 12th Edition* (Edited by M. Craft).

On behalf of all the participants, we thank the Bishop Bekkers Foundation, Holland for creating the opportunity to meet together in the European Seminar, on whose proceedings this volume is based.

SECTION ONE: BACKGROUND

INTRODUCTION

Peter Mittler and Helen McConachie

This book is based on a European Seminar on the theme of 'Approaches to Parental Involvement' which was held at the University of Manchester in the autumn of 1981. It was sponsored by the Bishop Bekkers Foundation in Utrecht, and jointly organised by the Bishop Bekkers Institute and the Hester Adrian Research Centre in association with the International League of Societies for Persons with Mental Handicap.

The idea for a European Seminar arose from Dr. Sandor Nemeth and Enno Felix of the BBl which, in addition to its research and development work in the Netherlands, is now stimulating international studies designed to advance knowledge and understanding of the needs of mentally handicapped people. In May 1980 the Institute organised a workshop on the needs of young mentally handicapped children in developing countries which, with the support of UNICEF, Rehabilitation International and other organisations, has now developed into a major international study involving 13 developing countries in different parts of the world.

Closer collaboration between professionals and parents of mentally handicapped people was chosen as the theme of the seminar because it was felt to be one of the most significant developments in the field of mental handicap, and one in which much could be gained by the exchange of experiences and constructive suggestions for change among people from different countries. Over and above this, however, we wanted the seminar to lead to new developments in each country represented. To this end, we suggested that participants from each country should identify one or two ways in which they could use what they learned in the seminar in order to introduce or stimulate some degree of change in their own communities.

With this end in view, two participants came to the seminar from each of nine European countries – generally one parent and one professional. The parents were nominated by the national parent societies, who were mostly members of the International League of Societies for Persons with Mental Handicap (ILSMH). In general, it was the parent who then nominated a professional 'partner', mostly teachers and social workers but also a psychiatrist and a physiotherapist. There were 23 participants from Austria, Belgium, Denmark, England, France, West Germany, Netherlands, Norway and Sweden. The Royal Society for Mentally Handicapped Children and Adults (MENCAP) was represented by Pauline Fairbrother (vice-chairperson), James Ross (director of Welfare Services) and John Chillag, chairperson of MENCAP's International Committee, and also of the European Committee of ILSMH.

Eleven papers were specifically written for the seminar and were circulated to all participants in advance. With the exception of a contribution from Canada, all the papers were prepared in Britain, six of these by members of research teams based in the Hester Adrian Research Centre (HARC) and the other five by parents and professionals from other areas.

Staff of HARC have for the past 11 years been involved in a variety of different approaches to working with parents (briefly summarised in *Parents' Voice*, vol. 29, pp.14-15, 1979). In 1970 and 1971 Cliff Cunningham and Dorothy Jeffree directed a series of informal evening workshops in which parents of pre-school mentally handicapped children were helped to assess the developmental level of their children and on this basis to help them to reach the next stage in their development. This led in 1973 to a four year research project in which Dorothy Jeffree and Roy McConkey developed a series of measures to help parents to assess their pre-school child's current abilities and also devised a large number of simple teaching games which were incorporated in a series of books published by Souvenir Press (eg. *Let Me Speak, Let Me Play, Teaching the Handicapped Child*). Cliff Cunningham's home visiting programme to Down's syndrome infants and their parents also began in 1973 and still continues. The Anson House Preschool Project was launched in 1975 and has developed influential models of practice in relation to the integration of handicapped and non-handicapped children and also in

4

respect of parental involvement. In 1977 Dorothy
Jeffree and Sally Cheseldine began the Parents and
their Handicapped Teenagers project by conducting a
survey of over 200 mentally handicapped school
leavers and their families in Greater Manchester;
they then developed a variety of approaches designed
to help these young people to extend the range of
both their leisure skills and their social interactions, partly through parental involvement.

These and other HARC projects reflect a variety
of different approaches to working with parents and
also reflect the exploration over the past ten years
of a variety of patterns of partnership. The
European seminar helped to widen our horizons and
has stimulated new developments.

The chapters that follow are based on edited
and adapted versions of the papers which were
presented at the seminar. In addition, we have
summarised the discussions following the presentation of each paper or group of papers; these were
led by teams from six of the countries, each of
which had made a particularly close study of the
papers before coming to Manchester, often in association with other colleagues in their own areas. We
have also prepared summaries of the accounts given
by participants of the situation concerning
relationships between parents and professionals in
their own countries or in their own immediate
localities. We also prepared edited versions of the
discussions which follow the papers.

The book is introduced by an 'overview' chapter
by Peter and Helle Mittler which tries to provide
definitions and a rationale for partnership between
parents and professionals, and which gives a number
of examples of specific ways in which such a
partnership can be realised at various stages of a
child's development. Particular attention is given
to the needs of parents of adolescents and young
adults. The following two chapters (Phillipa
Russell and James Ross) are by parents in positions
of leadership in voluntary organisations, the first
summarising parents' needs and the second illustrating one way in which parents have helped and
supported each other.

The next four chapters illustrate a variety of
approaches to partnership in the early years of
childhood. Dana Brynelsen describes a government-
supported home visiting programme for developmentally delayed children in British Columbia.
Cliff Cunningham reports on a home visiting project
for families of Down's syndrome children in the

first two years of life, starting as young as six
weeks. Sally Beveridge describes a university-based
integrated facility for mentally handicapped and
normally developing pre-school children, where
parents are fully involved in all decision-making
concerning the child's individual programme and
attempts are made to understand and meet the needs
of the child in the wider context of the family.
Helen McConachie's chapter discusses how these and
other families of young handicapped children
perceive their roles as parents and siblings and how
widely individual families differ in their organization of daily life at home.
      Relationships between parents and teachers of
school age children are then explored in three contrasting chapters. Barbara Smith literally provides
an A-Z of the various elements of partnership
between teachers and parents. Shirley Rheubottom's
chapter illustrates some of the difficulties of
developing such a partnership when the authorities
provide a transport service which unwittingly
distances parent and teacher, and the child from
other children. Jill Gardner provides a detailed
account of how one school gradually modified its
relationships with parents in a series of workshops
in which parents were helped to become proficient in
specific teaching skills within the context of
curriculum objectives set by the school.
      Relationships between professionals and parents
develop new dimensions and new problems as children
become adolescents and young adults. Dorothy
Jeffree and Sally Cheseldine illustrate some of
these in the context of a survey of the social
abilities and leisure interests of a group of young
people about to leave special schools, which highlighted the vital importance of parents and teachers
sharing their knowledge and skills at this crucial
time. Pauline Fairbrother takes this a step further
by considering some of the basic questions facing
young adults and their families, including those
concerned with the development of adult sexuality
and the need to prepare adults for separation from
their parents and for their eventual death.
      The last section of the book looks to the
future. First, Helen McConachie summarises reports
from European participants concerning relationships
between parents and professionals in their countries
which indicate clearly that, in some countries, at
least, particularly the Netherlands and Sweden,
parents have consciously decided against close
partnership, preferring to leave teaching to

6

teachers and to be free to concentrate on their role
as parents. Other countries report a range of
relationships, some involving open conflicts and
some working painfully towards collaboration. For a
British audience, it was particularly interesting to
hear accounts of teachers employed in schools
established by parent organizations and supported
from public funds.

Finally, Peter Mittler summarises possibilities
for progress. Some of these were drawn from the
plans prepared by participants themselves during the
course of the seminar, in fulfillment of the aim of
'putting the seminar to work' by developing an
action plan for implementation in their own
communities. Others arose from the papers and from
discussions following the papers.

We are publishing this book because we learned
a great deal from the seminar. It was refreshing
to meet people from other countries and to be able
to share ideas and experiences in small groups. We
learned that although we have a great deal in
common in terms of many of the basic questions
which confront anyone working and living with
mentally handicapped people, there are also many
major differences in attitudes and approaches - to
being a parent, to being a professional and to the
range of possible relationships between the two.
The fact that parents and professionals came 'in
pairs' meant that at least some of them had already
established some kind of working relationship
before they arrived. But many of them found that
hearing about the rich variety of possible relationships caused them to re-examine their own and to
listen with special interest to accounts which
differed radically from their own experience.

There is clearly no prescription for partnership, just as there is no prescription for how to
be a parent or a teacher. Although some professionals are aware of how much there is to gain by
working in closer collaboration with parents,
parents in their turn should not feel forced to
collaborate and should have the right to 'opt out'.
Just as children are seen as unique individuals, so
parents must also be seen as individuals with
unique personalities and needs. But for those who
are prepared to explore what is involved in working
together, there is much to be learned from the
experience of others. We hope that this book will
make a contribution to the development of partnership and to meeting the needs of children and
adults who are mentally handicapped.

Chapter 1

PARTNERSHIP WITH PARENTS: AN OVERVIEW

Peter and Helle Mittler

INTRODUCTION

The development of better working relationships
between parents and professionals constitutes one of
the most significant developments in the field of
special education during the past decade. But
although a whole series of reports from government,
professional and parents' bodies endorse the principle, we have remarkably little information on actual
practice. Despite the positive climate of opinion
on the desirability of closer partnership between
parents and professionals, there is still considerable uncertainty about what to do and how to start.
     This chapter explores some of the elements in-
volved and provides examples of ways in which
partnership has been realised. An attempt will be
made to define and provide a rationale for partnership, and to illustrate different patterns of
collaboration. Examples will be given of relevant
service provision at various stages of the child's
development, including infancy, the pre-school,
school and school-leaving period. A more detailed
account will be given of special issues arising from
collaboration between professionals and parents of
adolescents and young adults, since these have received relatively little attention in the literature
so far. Finally we will attempt a summary of some
of the essential elements of partnership in the
light of our discussion of current practice.

APPROACHES TO PARTNERSHIP

We begin by drawing a distinction between parental
involvement and partnership. Parents may be productively involved in the work of professionals and
collaborate with schools and other institutions but

8

this may fall a long way short of partnership. We can think of partnership as an ideal, a goal towards which we should be working but one which is not necessarily achieved in practice, even when parents and professionals seem to be working well together.

Three main phases can be detected in the relationship of professionals and parents of handicapped children. For many years parents received little help from professionals and were left largely unsupported. Such advice as they received tended to be negative and rarely included practical suggestions on what they could do to help their child at home. Indeed, parents were at one time frequently advised to place the child in residential care.

The second phase, called the 'transplant' phase by Jeffree (1980) and beginning towards the end of the 1960s, took the form of training parents to use some of the techniques restricted to professionals and regarding them as 'co-therapists' or co-teachers. Many parents were quick to learn these techniques and put them to good use with their children; research workers began to investigate the most effective methods of training parents and enlisting their help in carrying out programmes devised by professionals (O'Dell, 1974). Professionals largely worked on the assumption that they knew best what the child should learn and therefore what the parents should do at home. It is not surprising that some parents rejected such a one-way approach and resented the implicit assumption that professionals knew what was best for their child.

We are now entering on a third phase which has been characterised as the 'consumer model'. This is summarised by Cunningham as follows:

> In the consumer model we ...... aim to augment parenting skills ...... and do not try to change the consumer (parent) into a professional teacher; we do not attempt to 'transplant' professional skills into the home so that professional therapies per se are maintained and extended via the parent. To do this is to risk 'rejection'. Instead, we offer parents what we feel is the necessary information for them to live with and help their child with Down's syndrome. They then select from this according to their current needs and in their own time.

> (Chapter 5, this volume)

The consumer model starts with the parents'
natural style of interacting with their child and
takes account of the needs, resources and uniqueness
of each individual family. It rests on the assumption that:

> .. further progress in developing services
> for young handicapped children is crucially
> dependent on understanding, and respecting,
> the range of different ways in which families
> think and live their lives. Approaches
> based merely on educational technology will
> fail to meet a child's or a family's needs,
> just as institutional answers failed prev-
> iously.

> (McConachie, Chapter 7, this volume)

Partnership involves a full sharing of knowledge, skills and experiences. A commitment to
partnership rests on the assumption that children
will learn and develop better if parents and
professionals are working together on a basis of
equality than if either is working in isolation.
One of the foundations of partnership between parents and professionals lies in the recogniton of how
much they have in common and how much they have to
learn from one another. In fact, it is not as easy
to make a sharp distinction between them as common-
sense might at first suggest. Professionals increasingly recognise that there is a parenting component to their work, and that a degree of emotional
involvement is essential. They must consider the
needs of the whole child and not just the need to
learn; they must build on their relationship with
the child in order to teach. Similarly, parents are
learning some of the technical skills of teaching,
such as breaking a task down into small steps, using
prompting, fading and reward techniques and so
on.
Perhaps we have all become a little intoxicated
in the past ten years by the success with which
many parents have responded to the opportunities
provided by professionals to share in the task of
working with their own child. It certainly is ex-
traordinary that it has taken so long for professionals to become aware of the many ways in which
parents can be actively enlisted in day to day work
with their child - so much so that the professionals
now write of parents, with some surprise, as 'the
only true experts', and 'the best resources we

have'. Perhaps the shortage of skilled staff and
the sudden drying up of public funds has caused them
to see the light. It may also be due in part to a
growing confidence among the professionals themselves, brought about by new developments in the
technology of teaching which not only lend themselves to communication to parents but which lose
much of their force if they are not shared with parents.

There is no doubt that many of the skills traditionally reserved for professionals can be learned
by parents and that there is a sense in which professionals need to learn to share some of their
skills with parents. But this is not necessarily a
reflection of partnership, though it is undoubtedly
a worthwhile and effective form of collaboration and
parental involvement. Partnership involves a two
way process of joint assessment and decision making
in which parents and professionals come together
right from the start.

Partnership can take many forms but it must by
definition be on a basis of equality, in which each
side has areas of knowledge and skill that it con-
tributes to the joint task of working with the
child. For example,

. it is not partnership when professionals
  unilaterally make their own assessments and
  decisions about what and how to teach the
  child and then ask the parents to co-operate
  in teaching the child or in keeping records
  to see whether he or she uses at home the
  skills that have been taught in school;
. it is not partnership when parents are shown
  how to carry out certain physical exercises
  without being given any intelligible explanations about the reasons why these particular exercises are necessary;
. it is not partnership when parents are not
  consulted about their own resources or
  abilities to collaborate even with teaching
  schemes that they themselves have helped to
  devise.

Partnership calls for an exploration of the
needs of the families, of their feelings about their
own competence and their own emotional and social
resources as a family. Parents of handicapped
people *have no common characteristics*; they come from all
sections of society and represent the whole range of
individual differences and personality. Profession-

als will therefore need to enlarge their own understanding of the tremendous variety of needs and the
infinite range of personalities which they will encounter in parents. They will need to strike a balance between helping parents to learn some of the
skills of professionals while at the same time helping them to retain their own sense of identity as
parents and as individuals.

Not all parents want to be involved in depth
and detail in the day to day task of teaching their
child, and even those who want to be involved may be
prevented from doing so by real practical obstacles
such as time, gross overcrowding, severe social or
marital problems or sheer exhaustion. If we are
serious about helping parents to choose, we must
allow them to choose not to be involved at the level
of detailed collaboration which some professionals
are now offering. After all, the level of work and
commitment to partnership with professionals is
still new in many places and quite unfamiliar to
some. Many parents still regard - or need to
regard - professionals as people with special training in working with handicapped children and as
possessors of all kinds of specialised techniques
which require three or more years training to
acquire. Having waited for several years for their
child to enter school, they need to believe that the
child is passing into the care of highly trained and
skilled professionals. It is therefore something of
a shock when they realise that teachers, like themselves, are often floundering and overwhelmed; they
may be unprepared for the opportunities for day to
day participation in assessing the child's needs and
in implementing daily programmes of collaborative
work.

A recent review by Turnbull and Turnbull
(1982), themselves both parents and professionals,
questions the extent to which parents really wish to
be involved in decision making and in joint teaching
with professionals. They review a number of studies
which reflect parents' frequently expressed wish to
be able to 'live their own lives'; to this end, what
they value most is competent teachers. When asked
to describe an ideal nursery school, only a few parents spontaneously mentioned parent involvement of
any kind as an essential component of the programme.
Furthermore, a number of studies cast doubt on the
actual quality of parents' participation in the
decision making process which is now a legal re-
quirement as a consequence of US Public Law 94-142.
In a survey of 2,300 parents from 438 school dist-

ricts in the USA, just over half the parents reported that their child's individual educational programme had been completed *before* the IEP meeting. Other studies reviewed by the Turnbulls indicate that teachers monopolised the conversation and that parents' contributions were largely confined to personal and family issues and were not about educational matters such as assessment, curriculum and placement.

The Turnbulls note the paradox that while special education has made progress in knowledge of how to meet the individual needs of children, it has not yet reached the stage where it allows for a sufficiently wide range of variation in the individuality of parents. This means that parents should feel free to choose not to be involved with a school programme.

> Rather than mandating that all parents be equal participants with the school personnel to make decisions jointly, public policy should tolerate a range of parent involvement choices and options, matched to the needs and interests of the parent.

A RATIONALE FOR PARTNERSHIP

A case for the development of a closer partnership between parents and professionals might include the following considerations (Mittler, 1979).

1. Growth and learning in children can only be understood in relation to the various environments in which the child is living. These include his or her immediate family, peers, schools, local community and the wider society. The study of child development calls for an examination of ways in which the child interacts with, affects and learns from these various environmental influences. We can neither study nor teach the child in isolation.

2. Teachers and parents have similar goals, particularly for the more severely handicapped. Thus, both teachers and parents will be concerned with ways of teaching the child self-care and social independence, including self-feeding, dressing and toileting, as well as early cognitive skills, symbolic and representational play and learning to understand and produce language. Social and emotional development are equally the concern of both teachers and parents.

3. Studies contrasting the relative influence of home and school on children's intellectual and

educational achievements strongly suggest that the
influence of the home is comparatively greater in
the early years and that children who come from
homes where the parents take an active interest in
the child's education tend to have higher school
attainments. These studies have for the most part
been carried out on normal children but there is
evidence that this relationship is likely to be even
stronger in handicapped children.

4.   Parents need to be aware of the precise
teaching methods and strategies being used by teachers and other professionals to achieve any particular teaching goal. It is important for parents and
teachers to adopt a reasonably consistent approach
in helping children to learn to feed or dress themselves, in encouraging the use of longer sentences
or in dealing with behaviour difficulties. Such
methods need to be discussed and agreed between
teachers and parents so that at the very least each
is familiar with the approach being taken by the
other.

5.   Mentally handicapped children have been
shown to have particular difficulties in general-
ising their learning experiences and to use in one
setting skills which they have learned in another.
Special measures are needed to overcome this def-
icit, including carefully planned programmes to
teach generalisation across settings.

6.   Knowledge and experience of normal children and ordinary parental intuition, while undoubtedly valuable, are not necessarily adequate to
assist the development of a handicapped child. It
is not enough for professionals to advise parents
to treat their handicapped child as they would any
other child. Such advice is well meaning but does
not go far enough in preparing parents for some of
the specific difficulties which they will experience
in meeting the needs of children whose development
is not proceeding normally or where there are severe
abnormalities and disorders of development or behaviour.

In the first place, the age of the handicapped
child is not always an adequate guide for the parent. Not only is the child likely to be developing
much more slowly than normal, but some areas of development may be proceeding more slowly than others.
It is important for the parent to be aware of the
significance of such uneven development, particularly, for example, in the area of speech and language development where underfunctioning is common.
Some parents are easily discouraged by lack of pro-

14

gress and need to appreciate the significance of
even the smallest step in development and the means
by which the child can be helped to attain it.

Furthermore, there is sometimes a risk that the
child remains for too long at a particular stage of
development because it is assumed that this is part
of the handicap. Parents and teachers need to work
together to plan the next developmental step and to
remain alert to signs from the child of readiness to
respond to teaching designed to help in the acquisition of new skills. When development takes place
in 'slow motion' or when it is distorted by severe
handicaps, it is particularly important to maintain
a regime of demand and expectation and not to assume
that all difficulties and problems are due to the
handicap when they may to some extent spring from
under-estimation of what can be expected of the
child or from teaching goals that are no longer
developmentally appropriate.

THE NEEDS AND STRENGTHS OF FAMILIES

It is all too easy to generalise about 'the needs of
families' and to overlook the enormous range of individual differences. These will differ as much as,
if not more than, the needs of any other families.
We should also beware of drawing too sharp a distinction between parents of handicapped and non-
handicapped people. For example, in studying the
families of cerebral palsied children, Hewett (1970)
concluded that "families meet the day to day problems that handicap creates with patterns of behaviour that in many respects deviate little from the
norms derived from studying the families of normal
children. They have more similarities with ordinary
families than differences from them" (page 194).
Most parents of handicapped people have also had
several other normal children, and will, therefore,
have considerable experience not only of child-
rearing, but also of helping their older children to
achieve independence. It surely makes sense to
harness the experience and expertise of parents in
bringing up their own children and in knowing the
needs and strengths of their handicapped child.

To stress the essential individuality and
normality of the families is not to deny the range
and severity of the problems they face; rather it
is to counter the assumptions and stereotypes which
have so often been used by professionals and researchers about the underlying social pathologies
to be found in the families. The danger lies in

the consequent lack of appropriate action by professionals in response to families' needs. For example, parents seeking help at an early stage report
being labelled 'overanxious' and denied credit for
close observation of their child (e.g. Schaefer,
1979). Families seeking residential care for their
handicapped member may be investigated for 'guilt'
and 'rejection'; those not seeking relief may be
labelled 'overprotective'. The behaviour of the
families may be interpreted as abnormal whatever
they do. Such negative stereotyped judgements are a
poor basis for partnership (Mittler, Cheseldine and
McConachie, 1981).

We need more information on how the family as
a whole perceive their needs and what kind of demands are made on other members of the family both
by the needs of the child and the expectations of
professionals. The emotional reactions and practical realities of all the individual members of the
family will determine the nature and degree of any
possible partnership between the family and professionals. While the training and experience of social
workers lays particular emphasis on the skills of
working with the family as a whole, all professionals working with families will need to be aware
of the normality of negative feelings and of the
problems of balancing the needs of the handicapped
person with those of other members of the family
and household.

We should also note that whatever we might say
about whole families, many mothers are in fact
looking after handicapped children largely on their
own and with little help or support from other
family members or from the surrounding community
(Wilkin, 1979). In addition, many children now
live with only one parent, generally the mother.
Unsupported mothers have special problems; although
special financial incentives in the form of grants
are available, these are rarely adequate to provide
help with the day to day task of looking after a
home and caring for and working with a handicapped
child. Furthermore, some mothers would prefer to
work at least part-time, just like mothers of other
children, and do not wish to be tied to the home or
to a programme of intensive care, however well
thought out. Here again, we need to find the means
of allowing mothers to express their own preferences, and to choose between rationally presented
alternatives.

Many people are also acting as parent substitutes: in particular foster parents, staff of resi-

dential care establishments, including hospitals, as well as children's hostels or group homes. Residential care workers are currently discussing the extent to which they should in fact see themselves as substitute parents; doubts are being expressed about the possibility or even the desirability of professional staff acting as parent substitutes at all.

It seems essential that residential care staff should become as skilled as parents have shown themselves to be in working in partnership with other professionals to achieve developmental goals and objectives for the children in their care. This means that residential care workers should be encouraged to work in partnership with schools, with assessment and development centres and clinics, with parents themselves, and with any other agencies whose job it is to assess and draw up developmental plans for handicapped children. It is ironic that professional residential care staff rarely seem to take part in the process of assessment and programme planning, when many parents have demonstrated their willingness and ability to contribute their expert knowledge of the child by acting to all interests and purposes as members of the assessment team. It might be argued that professional staff should expect to be involved in both assessment and programme planning, and that they should be trained to acquire the necessary skills to do so.

In addition to partnership between professionals and parents in relation to their own child, we should also emphasise the growing participation by parents in policy formation at local, national and international levels. Parents are increasingly participating in decision making affecting the planning, development and operation of services. At local level, for example, more parent representatives will in future be acting as school governors, as members of community health councils and as members of joint care planning teams which have been established since 1976 to work for more effective collaboration between health and local authorities. Of course, there are still many parts of the country where parents are excluded from such bodies as a matter of policy but the movement for participation is growing.

At national level, parent representatives have worked effectively on a number of influential government advisory bodies - for example, on the Warnock Committee and the National Development Group for the Mentally Handicapped; they also take part in

visits to field authorities by the Development
Team for Mental Handicap. At the international
level, the International League of Societies for
Persons with Mental Handicap - a federation of 85
parent and professional societies in 65 countries -
was not only responsible for the drafting of the UN
Declaration of Rights of the Mentally Handicapped in
1971 but has since published detailed guidelines on
how these rights can be implemented in services
(ILSMH, 1978). It is also very active in working
with the UN international agencies, such as WHO,
UNICEF, UNESCO and ILO.

EXPRESSIONS OF PARENT-PROFESSIONAL COLLABORATION

Collaboration with parents is, then, one of the
hallmarks of a well trained professional. Shelter-
ing behind the walls of the organisation is a sign
of professional insecurity, an indication that they
are unsure of what they are doing or where they are
going and are unable to share their concerns with
those who care most about the handicapped person.
     We can now consider a number of examples of
collaboration between professionals and parents.
Many of these examples are already in operation or
are accepted in principle. Some are blocked for
financial or administrative reasons; others cannot
be implemented because of local attitudes and practices. Few call for significant new expenditure but
all demand a commitment to working in closer partnership with parents (see also Pugh (1981) for
other examples).

At Birth or Early Identification
Recent events have underlined the importance of ensuring that each maternity unit should develop procedures for the communication of the diagnosis of
handicap to parents and should consider how this
should best be handled. Although it is impossible
to offer guidelines which would have general valid-
ity, there is ample evidence to indicate that the
manner in which the diagnosis of handicap is first
communicated to parents is of such profound importance for the development of the relationship between
parent and child and between parents and professionals that it deserves the most serious study at
local level. Current evidence suggests that this
matter is still all too often handled with an
absence of sensitivity to parents' feelings.
     The balance of evidence from several surveys

18

indicates that the majority of parents want to be informed of the diagnosis within the first 48 hours, in the presence of both parents and of the child but not in front of other hospital staff or students. They also want access to accurate information and opportunities to ask questions at subsequent meetings with the doctor. Above all, the parents want practical support and guidance after leaving hospital (Spain and Wigley, 1975; Cunningham and Sloper, 1977).

However well the early communication of handicap is handled, it is essential to provide several opportunities for parents to discuss their reactions and to ask questions at leisure. Parents should also be given a leaflet which briefly lists the names and addresses of the main statutory and voluntary agencies that may be able to help. Parents will not necessarily wish to avail themselves of the offer of help at this stage but the opportunity to do so at a later stage should be made available by providing the relevant information in written form to enable them to do so if they wish. Many parents also welcome a written explanation of their child's diagnosis and a factual statement of its possible implications, together with some indication of the forms of help that can be offered by the hospital. In an increasing number of areas, an experienced parent makes contact with the new parents, sometimes accompanied by a health visitor or social worker.

Hospital staff are not always well informed about community support services for parents or children. For example, they may be unaware of parents' self help groups, of 'parent to parent' programmes, of fostering, adoption and respite care schemes developed by social services departments or voluntary organisations. Nor are they necessarily aware of the rapid developments which have taken place in schools and in the development of methods of teaching even the most severely handicapped children. As a result, an unduly gloomy prognosis may be given which does not necessarily match up with the development of services to young handicapped children and their families.

Children under Five
The 1981 Education Act marks a distinct advance in recognising the importance of parents' access to information and services right from the start. Amongst its most important provisions are the following:
    1.   Local Education Authorities are given the

powers to assess the special educational needs of children under two, if the parents agree, and are required to make such an assessment if the parents request it (Section 6).

2. Health Authorities have a duty to inform both the LEA and the parents of any children under the age of five who are likely to have special educational needs. They must also provide opportunities to discuss with parents any decision to notify the LEA, though parents cannot prevent this (Section 10).

3. Health Authorities also have a duty to inform parents of the name of the appropriate voluntary organisation that may be able to help them (Section 10).

Where children with special needs are attending integrated forms of provision, it is particularly important to ensure that the needs of their parents are not overlooked. Many children are attending ordinary pre-school services, such as nursery schools and classes and playgroups but this does not mean that parents are given opportunities to participate on a basis of equality and partnership in the making of decisions about their child's day to day programme of activities.

Whenever possible one person should provide a 'single point of contact' for families, to act as their source of support and, where necessary, of advocacy to help to ensure that decisions taken by service agencies are implemented and regularly reviewed. Services for the family should be mediated by this person, to avoid duplication and the risk of contradictory advice and misinterpretation. In a sense, he or she acts as a co-ordinator and communicator between professionals, as well as providing support for the family. They should also mediate between the family and professionals - for example, in helping the family to express their dissatisfaction with the programmes being developed for their child or in indicating that the pressure either on the child to learn or on the family to participate may be imposing excessive strain.

A home-visiting service at the earliest possible moment should always be available. It is not enough to ask parents to bring their baby to a paediatric or 'well baby' clinic. Many parents do not feel sufficiently at ease in these situations to enter into terms of equality with professionals. Parents who brought their children to such centres, often with considerable inconvenience to themselves and distress to their children, have frequently ex-

pressed disappointment at the outcome. Although the
child was generally expertly assessed, sometimes by
multidisciplinary teams including not only doctors
but psychologists, speech and physiotherapists and
perhaps an educationalist or social worker, it was
relatively rare for the parents to be given any
advice or assistance on how they themselves could
actively work with their child at home to further
his or her development. They might be given general
advice, along the lines of 'treat your child as
normally as possible' or 'talk to him and play with
him as much as you can' and told to come back in so
many months so that the specialists could monitor
the child's development. But they were not necessarily shown particular and specific approaches that
might be helpful - for example, methods of holding
and carrying a child with cerebral palsy, how to
overcome feeding problems presented by a severely
handicapped child, by a child with Down's syndrome
who was exceptionally slow to feed, perhaps due to
a large tongue or weak musculature, or how to help
a child to learn to communicate.

Examples of a home visiting service for parents
of preschool children can be found in the Portage
programmes, developed initially in rural areas in
the USA but now successfully replicated in the UK
(Revill and Blunden, 1980). The model here is one
in which a home visitor (who can be trained in as
little as a week) visits families once a week in
order to work out short term goals for the child and
to introduce specific structured methods which the
parents can use to try to help the child to reach
such goals within one or two weeks. (See Chapter 4,
this volume.)

Regular visits to the home also provide opportunities for the parent to raise wider issues beyond
the immediate training programme - for example, problems or anxieties about future school placement,
entitlements to allowances and benefits or questions
concerned with the needs of other members of the
family, particularly siblings. While the home
visitor will be able to provide a considerable
amount of support to the family in raising and discussing these issues, she or he will need to have
sufficient knowledge of other agencies to know
whether outside help should be sought. (See Chapter
5, this volume, and Cunningham and Sloper, 1978.)
Even so, it is dangerous to assume that it will
always be possible for parents to adopt a teaching
role with their child. Discussions of a frank and
open nature about what is appropriate and possible

for each family is essential if we are to avoid the risk of imposing both practical and emotional burdens on families.

Partnership between Home and School
The range of relationships between parents and teachers is very wide. It can extend, at one extreme, from merely formal communication about dates of terms to open access to all reports and records on their child, to participation of parents in classroom teaching, discussions of school policy and curriculum and selection of teachers as members of school governing boards.

Many schools are now re-examining their practice, just as many parents are pressing for a greater degree of participation in the development of plans and programmes for their own child. In particular, parents who have had positive and successful experiences of collaboration with professionals before their child went to school represent a new generation of articulate, well informed and highly skilled parents. Once their child moves into full-time special education, they tend to ask questions about the school's policy for partnership with parents. "How are we going to work together in assessing my child's strengths, weaknesses and needs? When do we discuss selection of priorities for teaching and what kind of communication link are we going to set up to keep each other informed?"

Although there are a growing number of published reports of specific projects, we are short of factual information on the nature and extent of home-school links either nationally or regionally. One of the few exceptions is a survey of all special schools in Manchester undertaken by the Manchester School Psychological and Child Guidance Service in which one of us (HM) has been involved. A detailed questionnaire was developed which formed the basis of a semi-structured interview with headteachers and other staff of all the 28 special schools in the City. The results of the survey have been reported elsewhere (H. Mittler, 1982). Here we shall illustrate a number of ways in which home-school links are being developed, using as a starting point some items from the questionnaire and suggestions made by a number of writers. (See also Chapters 8 and 10, this volume.)

The Manchester questionnaire explored home-school links at three stages - when children first enter the school, while they are at school, and at the time of preparation for leaving. It also in-

22

vited suggestions from headteachers on ways in which parents can and do contribute to the life of the school and asked for examples of successful and less successful attempts to involve parents. As a result of this exercise, some headteachers approached parents about their own experience of collaboration with schools and invited suggestions from them on how home-school links could be improved. One new headteacher designed her own 36 item questionnaire, personally visited all the families of children in her school and is modifying school practice in the light of parents' responses (Boucher, 1981).

Entry into School
1. <u>Home visits</u> *Does a member of the school staff visit the family at home before the child starts school?*
Such visits enable the head or class teacher to get to know the whole family not just the mother, and to see the child in the home setting. They can help teachers to learn something of the child's behaviour at home, and to begin to build up a picture of strengths and needs, as well as the priorities of the family. An initial visit can also help to identify the best ways for the child to start school - e.g. by periods of part-time attendance, the extent to which a parent should stay with the child, any special difficulties about eating, toileting, medical problems and transport.

One of the aims of a home visit is to begin to discuss with the family ways in which home and school can establish a working relationship. This will obviously take time to negotiate and will depend on the resources and priorities of the family but visits to the home can begin to lay the foundations for a realistic discussion of what will and will not be possible. This is also a good opportunity to make it clear that parents are welcome at school.
2. <u>Assessment</u>. The 1981 Education Act formalises the rights of parents to be involved in decisions concerning their child's special educational needs. These rights are summarised in DES Circular 8/81 but further regulations and guidance are promised. Amongst the changes in the new Act are the following:

      1.   LEA's must notify parents of their intention to make an assessment and provide information about assessment and procedures. They must also notify parents of the results of the assessment. Parents must be given the name of an officer from whom

they can obtain further information and be informed about their rights of appeal to the Secretary of State.

2. Parents must receive a draft of the LEA's statement of special educational needs and have a right to an interview with an officer of the LEA and with anyone who gave advice to the LEA about their child's statement of needs. The LEA must consider any representations made by parents.

3. Parents have the right of appeal to a local appeal committee against special educational provision specified in a statement. Although the appeal committee can refer an appeal for the reconsideration of the LEA, they do not have the power to overrule the LEA. In this case, or if the appeal committee agree with the LEA's judgement, the parents can appeal to the Secretary of State if they are not satisfied with the LEA's decision. He or she has the power to confirm or amend the statement or to direct the LEA to cease to maintain the statement.

4. LEA's have a duty to comply with requests for assessments made by parents, 'unless it is in their opinion unreasonable'. Parents may appeal to the Secretary of State if they feel aggrieved by the LEA's decision not to make an assessment.

5. Parents are required to present the child for any examination felt necessary to enable the Secretary of State to determine issues arising from the provisions of the Act.

Once the child is in school, collaboration between parents and teachers is a matter of good practice rather than legislation. The question can therefore be put as follows:
How are the parents involved in the assessment of their child's skills, abilities and needs?
The answer to this question will depend on the kind of assessment procedures used in the school. Some schools use published developmental checklists, others have developed their own checklists. In either case, it is worth considering ways in which parents can provide information based on their own expert knowledge of the child's behaviour. Some schools go through a checklist with the parents item by item, others leave a copy of the list with the

parents and ask them to fill it in (perhaps each
parent doing so independently); others leave the
parents to study the questionnaire and then go over
it with them either at home or at school. Discrepancies between the assessments of parents and
teachers can form a productive starting point for
discussion, since it is not uncommon for certain
behaviours to be more in evidence in one setting
than another; for example, a child may put on his
own shoes at home and not at school, or vice versa.
Several studies have shown that parents' and
teachers' assessments correspond fairly closely when
they use the same instruments.

Do parents see records or have an opportunity to comment on
the observations of teachers towards the end of the initial
period of assessment and before their implications for further
teaching are considered by the school?

Once the school has completed its initial assessment, perhaps sometime during the first term, parents should be given an opportunity to discuss the
interim findings, to contribute their own observations and to comment on anything which they feel
might give a misleading impression of their child's
behaviour. Where there is genuine disagreement
about some aspect of a child's behaviour, the parents' observations should be recorded and noted,
with their knowledge.

For involvement of parents in the initial process of observation and assessment and in the
resulting formulation of the child's programme is of
the first importance. Parents should have the
opportunity to identify and discuss their priorities
for the child and to share with school staff the
methods that they have found helpful and unhelpful
in their own experience of the child at home. This
is also a good time to discuss ways in which
teachers and parents are going to continue to communicate and to keep each other informed about the
child's progress and further needs. It is this
initial period that lays down the foundations for
later collaboration and trust. It is only if parents know and understand what their child is learning and doing at school that they can support and
work productively with teachers.

During School Years
Collaboration between parents and teachers can take
a very wide variety of forms during the child's
years in school. The nature and quality of collaboration will vary with the changing needs of the
child, the parents and the teachers. Relationships

between home and school must therefore be flexible and must be able to respond to changing circumstances and the different responses of different families. There is clearly no set formula for partnership.

The questions and suggestions that follow merely represent some examples of current practice. We are not suggesting that all of them should apply in every school and for all children. But we do suggest that each school should consciously think out its policies and practices in relation to the development of partnership with parents. (See Chapter 8, this volume, for further examples.)

1. Access to school staff. Many headteachers say that 'parents are welcome in my school at any time'. What does this mean in practice? Can they go straight to the child's teacher or are they expected to talk to the headteacher first? What about access to other school staff? Are they clear about procedures for contacting staff? Should they telephone for an appointment first? What facilities are there for parents while they are waiting to see a member of staff? Many parents find it difficult or even stressful to stand or sit about with nothing to do and this can discourage them from visiting the school.

2. School meetings. Most schools arrange meetings of parents for a wide variety of purposes. Nearly all parents can visit schools at set times to look at displays of childrens' work and attend Christmas plays but these are really open days rather than meetings called for specific purposes - e.g. to discuss children's work and progress, sometimes following the preparation of the school report.

Meetings are held to provide opportunities for parents to meet visiting specialists such as physiotherapists, speech therapists, psychologists or doctors, not only to talk about their child but also to learn more about the work of these specialists and how they relate to teachers. Some schools also hold meetings to discuss important educational issues, such as possible changes in the policy of the school, aspects of the curriculum, methods of teaching, changes in services or legislation, new developments in services for adolescents or adults.

In addition to meetings for parents as a whole, some schools make it possible for small groups of parents to meet either informally or for a particular purpose. For example, some schools have a special parents' 'den' where they can meet at any time, make hot drinks and simply chat, and where

meetings can be held to discuss particular issues.
The actual physical arrangements for parents to wait
are important if parents are to feel both comfortable and welcome when they visit the school.
3.   Review meetings. Many schools now hold regular
meetings to review the progress of each child and
some invite parents to attend either the whole or
part of such a meeting. Such meetings can be particularly productive where schools have developed a
detailed curriculum plan with recording systems
which enable both teachers and parents to provide
information on the child's progress in reaching
specific goals. Furthermore, the 1981 Education Act
gives parents the right to take part in annual
meetings to review the child's progress.
4.   Sharing success. Some teachers invite parents
into school to see the child at various stages of a
programme designed to teach a specific skill. The
parent is involved in planning and, if possible,
carries on some of the teaching at home. Emphasis
on achievements rather than problems can provide a
good foundation for partnership between parent, professional and child.
5.   Asking the parents. There are many ways in
which schools can approach individual parents
directly. Most commonly, they may make a special
point of discussing a particular problem presented
by the child and working out ways in which they can
jointly work towards a solution. This can be done
by inviting the parents into the school, by a visit
to the home or by a combination of the two.
   Quite apart from questions concerned with an
individual child, teachers may find it helpful to
discuss a range of general issues with individual
parents. These might concern questions of school
policy, organisation or curriculum, or a change
which is under consideration but which has not yet
been decided. Some schools have also taken the initiative in asking parents about their preferences
for receiving reports, information from the school,
social and informal meetings that would interest
them, contacts with school and visiting staff and
with other parents. Parents are more likely to feel
involved in the work of the school as a whole if
staff take them into their confidence about wider
questions of policy.
   It is also worth asking whether enough opportunities are available for parents to offer any
special interests or skills to the school. Some
schools wait for the initiative to be taken by the
parents, others ask parents directly or make

suggestions based on their own knowledge of parents' special interests. The range of possibilities among any group of parents must be very wide - it can include participating in extra-curricular activities, swimming, school visits or a particular skill or interest, such as cooking or carpentry, drama or other hobbies.

Residential Schools
Where a child is attending a residential school, partnership between parents and school staff presents obvious difficulties. Despite the special challenges involved, there is scope for considerable progress.

The number of children and families involved is not considerable. According to the most recent DES statistics relating to the year 1979 (DES, 1981), around one sixth of all pupils receiving special education in 1979 were in some form of residential school (not counting hospital schools). The majority of pupils in maintained and non-maintained residential schools were classified as ESNM (6165), followed by maladjusted (3951), and by either delicate or physically handicapped or both (3708). Comparable figures for independent schools are not available, though it is likely that many of the pupils with special educational needs would be classified as maladjusted.

The number of children in residential schools must be falling rapidly as a consequence of the financial problems facing local authorities. Many LEA's are either closing or reducing the numbers of children in residential schools for which they have a direct responsibility or are no longer able to pay the fees of children attending schools run by other LEA's or by private or voluntary organisations.

The withdrawal of children from residential schools clearly poses special problems of relationships with parents, particularly where the LEA proposes to return the child to the parental home. If the staff of the residential school and of the placing LEA have worked closely with the parents throughout the child's stay in the school, the foundations for effecting a smooth return to the family home or to a substitute home may well have been laid. Where this has not happened, the upheaval resulting from the closure of a residential school can be deeply harmful both to the child and the family and can adversely affect the development of both.

There should be clearly agreed procedures within the LEA and between its officers and the parents about how links between home and school are to be established and maintained. Clearly, the needs of families and children will vary widely, and will also change significantly over time, so that detailed guidelines would not be appropriate. But whether one LEA is involved, whether the placing LEA needs to relate to another LEA in which the residential school is situated, or to the staff of a non-maintained or independent school, the questions that need to be asked are essentially similar. We will list merely a few of the more obvious ones here, since most of the issues already discussed in relation to day special schools and classes apply in varying measures to residential schools also.

1. *How far do parents have the information on the range of possible schools at the time when the issue of boarding education is first raised?*

2. *Do all parents have an opportunity to visit possible schools? Who goes with them - a professional person responsible for the placement such as a social worker or educational psychologist or advisor?*

3. *How far are decisions on the choice of school in the hands of administrative staff? In that case, what opportunities are there for parents to discuss choice of schools with them?*

4. *When parents visit the school to discuss possible placement, do they meet the whole range of staff or only the headteacher?*

5. *If the child's admission to school is likely, does a member of the school staff visit the family at home? If so, do they also liaise with staff of the child's previous school and the agencies responsible for the placement - e.g. school psychological or child guidance service?*

6. *Once the child is in school, what kind of communication links are envisaged between home and school?*

7. *Is there a step by step plan either to return the child to his family or to make alternative arrangements (e.g. fostering, hostel)? In the latter case, how are the parents informed of a decision to seek alternative forms of care?*

8. *While the child is in residential school, who works with the family - is it local staff (e.g. school psychological, child guidance, social services) or staff of the residential school or both? What happens in school holidays?*

9. *How do those responsible for the placement*

decision monitor the child's progress and the appropriateness of their recommendations and choice of school?

10. *How does the placing and paying LEA satisfy itself that the school is meeting the needs of the children they have placed there? Do they regularly visit the school or do they ask an officer of the LEA in which the school is situated to do so? Who visits - psychologist, teacher, social worker, administrator?*

11. *Within any one residential school, what arrangements have been made to develop effective communication concerning the needs of the child and how these will be met jointly between teaching and residential care staff? Are all school staff responsible to the headteacher or are residential care staff responsible to someone else, either inside or outside the school? To what extent do residential care staff help to share in decision making and planning - e.g. through case conferences and review meetings?*

Most of the questions we have raised could also be asked in those situations where children attend a day school but are living in a hostel or small group home. This is not uncommon in the case of ESNS schools; children may be living in a hostel attached to or close to the school, sometimes for five days, sometimes for the whole week. In this situation, the three-way relationship between parents, school and residential care staff can become quite complex and requires very careful handling.

Preparation for Leaving School
Although much has been written about the need for careful and detailed assessment of the abilities and needs of school leavers, we have little information about the involvement of parents in the process of assessment and decision making involved. As we discuss this matter in detail below, we will merely list a number of questions at this stage.
How far are parents involved in the planning and actual implementation of the school's curriculum for leavers?
Since parents will in many cases assume complete responsibility for the care of the young person, it is obviously essential to learn about their own concerns and priorities and to work for the fullest possible partnership at this critical time.
Are parents involved in the assessment process?
In order to build up a comprehensive profile of all the young person's abilities it is essential to draw

on the parents' knowledge of what he or she can do
at home. In a study of 214 mentally handicapped
school leavers. Cheseldine and Jeffree (1982)
showed that the Pathways to Independence Checklist
was realiably used by most parents, even though very
few had previously been given opportunities to complete a developmental checklist on their child.
Do teachers visit the family at home?
Home visits to both parents (and to other members of
the family living in the household) are particularly
important at this time not only to elicit the parents' knowledge of what their child can do but also
to learn about their own priorities, needs and resources.
*Do parents attend any case conferences held to discuss their
child's future?*
Not all schools hold case conferences and parents
are not necessarily invited to attend those that are
held. Sometimes they are only invited in on a
'token basis' once the decisions have been made.
*Do parents have opportunities to talk individually to profess-
ionals involved in the assessment process or in the provision
of future services?*
These might include the educational psychologist,
careers officers, social worker, adult training
centre manager, staff of further education college
or one of the courses run by the Manpower Services
Commission, doctors, speech therapists or physiotherapists.
*How much of a say does the young person have in the process of
decision making and what happens where the opinion of the
young person and those of the parnets are clearly at variance?
Are there parent workshops and discussion groups specifically
for parents and school leavers?*
Some schools have held such workshops with the
specific aim of developing a consistent approach to
helping pupils acquire community living skills and
of ensuring that skills that are learned in one
setting, whether at home or school, are not only
used in the other but also in 'real' situations in
the community. Such joint approaches have been used
to help young people to use public transport, self
service cafes, sport and recreational facilities.
In addition to specific training objectives, workshops and discussion groups have also been held to
explore questions concerned with personal and sexual
relationships, family problems and disagreements
between the young person and family or teachers.
*How much do parents know and see of the self-help and inde-
pendence skills that their child is being taught at school?
What steps have to be taken to link such teaching with what*

the parents are doing at home?

PARENTS OF ADOLESCENTS AND YOUNG ADULTS[1]

The period of school leaving marks a critical point
in the life of the family as well as that of the
adolescent. But although there is now a considerable literature about parents of younger handicapped
children, very little is known about families of
handicapped adolescents and young adults. How far
do such families have special and distinctive needs?
To what extent do the roles of parents of handicapped adolescents differ from the role of parents
of younger children, both those who are handicapped
and those who are not? What kind of services do
families need to help them to fulfil their role?

Some Service Needs of Parents
The time of school leaving provides an opportunity
to take stock not only of the needs of the young
person but also those of the family. Families
should feel that there is time and opportunity to
discuss any aspects of their family life which concerns their son or daughter either now or in the
future. Such discussions need not be limited to the
immediate questions arising from school leaving and
placement into adult services. Both parents and
professionals are increasingly expressing the wish
to move away from a crisis-orientated service towards one which anticipates needs and tries to plan
constructively to meet them. For example, parents
should be given the opportunity to discuss questions
concerned with residential care long before there is
a direct need for it.

Information. First and foremost, parents need information on the range of provision which is available
or planned in their locality. In interviews with
parents in one area where services were well developed, many parents were badly informed about day or
residential services for adolescents and adults.
Very few had visited the Adult Training Centres
which their children would almost certainly be
attending in the coming months (Cheseldine and
Jeffree, 1982). They were also poorly informed
about facilities for short-term and longer-term residential care in their localities. Lack of information was more common among parents who were not
members of parents' societies or who did receive
the parent journals in which such issues are regularly discussed.

32

A number of authorities have been producing
short information leaflets on local services.   These
generally contain addresses and telephone numbers of
key organisations and individuals as well as useful
information on where to get advice or help to meet
particular needs.   These leaflets are often aimed at
parents of younger children; there is a case for an
information sheet written especially for parents of
young people approaching school leaving age.   This
might include information on the following:

- local provision for assessment of young people
  approaching school leaving age - e.g. which
  professions should be routinely involved in
  assessment and decision-making and which
  others are available for consultation if the
  need should arise;
- procedures for parents to be involved in the
  process of assessment and decision-making; how
  and when they should be consulted; how they
  can obtain the information or advice which they
  feel to be necessary and whom to contact if
  they are dissatisfied;
- the range of alternative provision which is
  available locally - e.g. day services, further
  education colleges, work experience courses,
  sheltered employment, vocational training.
  This should include the names of key individuals in these organisations who can advise
  parents and who might be able to arrange for
  preliminary visits to the agency;
- the range of residential services - both long
  term and short term - should also be summarised
  in such a leaflet, together with some indication on how parents can visit facilities informally;
- information on welfare rights for which the
  young person and the family are eligible;
- in addition to listing services for handicapped
  people, such leaflets should also include information on all relevant resources available
  to the rest of the community and to young
  people in particular - e.g. careers advice,
  work training, further education facilities,
  evening classes and the whole range of leisure,
  sport and recreational facilities in the area.

Anticipating needs for residential and support services
Information leaflets may provide the basis for an
informed discussion between parents and professionals on the availability of local resources.   For

example, parents often express the need not only to be told about the local services that are available or planned but also to have the opportunity to discuss the advantages of the various alternatives in relation to the needs of their son or daughter and of the family as a whole.

Discussion about the range of alternatives may also provide opportunities for families to express more general feelings about their attitudes and needs. To this end, it is obviously desirable that there are opportunities to relate to a single individual, preferably someone with experience of working with families.

For example, a quick and superficial visit to the family may well result in a report that the family are unwilling to consider residential care. But several visits and the development of a more open and trusting relationship may help the parents to speak more freely about the problems in continuing to provide 24 hour care and may make them less hesitant to express their wish to think about residential care outside the home.

Similarly, some parents may refer to arrangements that have been made for an older brother or sister to make a home for the handicapped youngster when the parents are no longer able to do so. This was mentioned quite frequently in interviews, particularly when many of the leavers are the youngest of a large family, with many brothers and sisters now married (Cheseldine and Jeffree, 1982). But parents may be reluctant to rely on their own children to take over care, though there is evidence that older siblings no longer living at home tend to give considerable help and are willing to take over. Bayley (1973) found that among mentally handicapped adults living in the community, 85 per cent of those who could be living with a sibling (i.e. both parents dead) were doing so, though of those in hospital, half had been admitted immediately after the death of a parent. But such an arrangement is not necessarily entered into willingly by the older brother or sister or their spouse; it may be made in order to reassure worried parents that the handicapped youngster will be taken care of when the time comes. Furthermore, circumstances can change, particularly in a growing family. For these and other reasons, it is important for the professional not simply to record that family arrangements have been made but to explore the situation in some depth and detail with the parents and the younger family involved.

34

In interviews in the Greater Manchester area,
we found few families of school leavers who were
well-informed about the residential services which
were available in their area. Many still assumed
that the long-stay mental handicap hospital was the
only alternative to remaining at home and were
unaware of existing and planned local authority provision for hostels and group homes. The movement
towards the use of ordinary housing for handicapped
people, although increasingly influential in professional circles, has not made the same impact on
individual families.

Using ordinary housing. Many parents expect to continue
to provide a home for their handicapped son or
daughter indefinitely, until they are no longer able
to do so by reason of age, incapacity or death. The
notion that young people might be given opportunities to live away from their families *before* there is
a crisis has as yet made relatively little headway.
This is partly due to the shortage of provision in
the community but is also related to the narrow
range of alternative accommodation which has until
recently been considered appropriate. This may
change, now that more consideration is being given
to the use of ordinary housing and evidence is
beginning to be published indicating that even
severely handicapped people can live in ordinary
houses.
    Providing ordinary or adapted housing in the
local community means that people can live in small
units with as much staffing and support as their
individual needs require. Some will require only a
very occasional visit from a social worker, health
visitor or voluntary worker; other houses may contain three to five more dependent people who will
need to have staff living in the house with them; in
other cases, professional staff live in a nearby
house but are available when needed. The emphasis
in such schemes is on providing a wide range of
residential accommodation to meet the wide range of
need of individuals.
    From the parents' point of view, such arrange-
ments provide ideal opportunities to help their sons
and daughters to learn to live more independently.
At the same time they can prepare themselves to
accept that although they will eventually need to
live away from home, such a home need not be a distant hospital or institution but a house not very
different from their own.
    Whether or not the young person is in regular

contact with professionals, parents can be given the
means to try to develop active teaching methods
which are designed to help the young person learn
new skills and to become more independent. Whelan
and Speake (1979) have written a handbook specifically for parents of mentally handicapped adolescents. Beginning with a *Scale for Assessing Coping
Skills*, parents are helped to complete a simple
checklist of the young person's abilities in the
areas of self-help (personal, domestic, community)
and interpersonal skills (e.g. conversation, friendship, sexual knowledge and behaviour). Detailed
suggestions are then made for ways in which parents
can design and carry out a teaching programme to
help the young person achieve specific skills. Such
an approach can also form the basis of structured
workshops in which groups of parents and professionals meet regularly in order to define short-term
goals and agree on methods of reaching them.

Because parents and professionals may not have
the same goals, it is important to provide opportunities for a free discussion to identify expectation of the level of independence that may be
achieved since these may differ widely in both
groups. Just as several professionals working with
the same adolescent may have different expectations
of the final outcome, so different members of the
same family may vary considerably in their estimate
of the extent to which the young person can learn
the skills to live successfully in the community.
It may therefore be helpful to explore these questions through discussion. It is clearly dangerous to
press ahead with carefully structured training programmes to teach social independence when one or
both parents may have misgivings about whether such
a programme is justified. They may also be anxious
about the risks involved in undertaking it.
Questions concerned with sexuality represent the
most obvious examples where full discussion about
goals and philosophies is important. Similarly,
parents and professionals may have different per-
ceptions about the extent to which a particular
youngster is 'ready' to start a course of social independence training - e.g. in learning to use public
transport, go to a supermarket or a disco unaccomp-
anied, go on holiday with a group of friends etc.

Special Problems of Partnership?
Are there distinctive problems about developing
partnership between parents of adolescents and
adults and the staff who work with them?

Even where parents and professionals are apparently agreed on the overall programmes for social independence training, difficult issues arise when it comes to discussing the nature and degree of parental participation in such programmes. Although there is now a strong body of evidence which testifies to the effectiveness of internsive parental involvement where teaching programmes with younger children are concerned, is it right to extrapolate these to parents of adolescents and young adults? How appropriate is such detailed involvement from a normalisation point of view? Is it appropriate that parents should know exactly what their son or daughter is doing in the course of their day to day social education or training programmes? Even very much younger children like to maintain separate identities between home and school and tend to fend off well meaning enquiries from parents about what they have been doing in school. It could be argued that even where such enquiries are not apparently resented and even where parents and professionals are working well together to achieve goals that are in the long-term interest of the adolescent, such a close involvement on the part of parents may in fact reinforce rather than diminish dependency.

These issues about goals and philosophies are not widely discussed in the literature, nor, we suspect, do they receive as much consideration as they should at the level of the individual family when professionals are beginning to draw up training programmes for handicapped young people. (See chapters 11 and 12, this volume.) Professionals may themselves need help in facing these issues; for example, group discussion, possibly accompanied by role play, may help staff to face some of the delicate and complex issues involved. Clearly, no two families have the same needs but certain general strategies can be discussed within a group. For example, some parental involvement programmes may begin with a fairly intensive and detailed level of training by parents but in the context of a clearly worked out plan to reduce the amount of parental involvement on a step-by-step basis. This can be done more easily with some programmes than others - e.g. in teaching a young person to travel to a day centre by public transport, the programme would probably consist of gradually 'distancing' the parent from the young person. Similarly, the amount and intensity of supervision in teaching a young person to wash their hair can also be slowly but systematically withdrawn.

Now that parents are being asked to enter into detailed and often day-to-day working partnerships with professional staff in teaching their son or daughter to acquire specific skills, it is particularly important to provide opportunities for them to express their feelings about any difficulties they may be experiencing in working in a teaching role. Some parents quite understandably find such work both demanding and stressful but may find it hard to admit to this, for fear of being thought unco-operative or not 'good parents'.

Preparation for adulthood also involves preparation for loss and separation. One of the greatest anxieties that parents face - even from the earliest days - is how their handicapped son or daughter will manage when parents are too old or too ill and when they die. These issues are often pushed aside 'taking each day as it comes'. But parents' and professionals' co-operation can be most valuable and mutually supportive in the joint task of helping the handicapped person and family to prepare for separation, both temporary and permanent. One of the most insightful and thought-provoking accounts of the meaning of the death of a parent to a mentally handicapped adult can be found in a work of fiction - *Walter*, by David Cook (Penguin Books, 1980).

CONCLUSIONS: THE ESSENCE OF PARTNERSHIP

Partnership between parents and professionals is an easily accepted principle but the constructive relationship it represents is much more difficult to achieve. It calls for considerable thought and effort on both sides.

What, then, are some of the essential elements that we look for in partnership?

1. *Mutual respect and recognition of the essential equality between parents and professionals*. Each has a deep interest and concern for the child. Each wants the best possible future for the child and works towards this in their own way. The parent is more deeply and intensely involved, more 'partial', as Elizabeth Newson puts it. Most parents have a life long commitment to the child and their responsibility lasts for 24 hours a day, during holidays and sickness. Professionals have, on the whole, a more finite commitment. Their work may be more specialised in nature - concerned with the education in a broad sense, speech and language, mobility, vocational training and so on. They may change jobs or work

with another group of children.

Nevertheless, the roles of parent and professional in the field of handicap are more than usually interactive and complementary. The warm and affectionate care of the parent and the physical help a parent offers will need to be maintained when children are aware from their parents; parenting needs to be carried on by professionals. Similarly, teaching to minimise the handicap needs to be carried on by the parents at home to a greater degree than when no handicap exists. This is particularly true of mentally handicapped children who need help to generalise the skills they have learned from one setting to another.

2. *Sharing of information and skills*. Parents have known and cared for their child since birth. They know intimately the child's idiosyncratic responses over a wide range of activities - eating, sleeping, elimination, playing, recognition of people, responses to sound, sights, likes, dislikes, fears. All parents will have experience of having helped their child to develop certain skills and will have gained valuable insights from their efforts. The parents will also know the social and physical environment in which the child lives and will continue to develop.

Professionals, for their part, have a background of knowledge derived both from their theoretical training and from the experience they have accumulated in working with a large number of handicapped children and their families. They will have learnt from their failures as well as their successes. Their experience helps them to acquire a range of methods and techniques to observe and assess strengths and needs and to help children to acquire skills and to increase independence.

It is vital for parents and professionals to share skills and information with each other, and to do so in an open, honest way which includes a sharing of each others' limitations in knowledge and expertise. This is not to deny that each has their own area of authority. This too needs mutual recognition and, hopefully, leads to the development of a common language and understanding without which little can be achieved together.

3. *Sharing of feelings*. Partnership can only be arrived at through a process of sharing. While practical skills and decisions may be the outcome of this process, the feeling element is at least equally important.

Traditionally, parents and professionals have

been wary of one another. They have come together with preconceived assumptions and ideas about each other and there is often an element of rivalry in their contacts. Inevitably, they lack confidence in how to approach one another: professionals rarely have preparation or training in ways of relating to parents. Parents often remember their own negative experiences of school and these experiences are reactivated when they meet teachers and other professionals.

Professionals can begin to meet parents on a personal level by being open about their own feelings. Sharing their initial reactions to handicap and early difficulties and failures may make parents more comfortable in expressing their own doubts and worries. Similarly, professionals and parents can help each other through difficult periods when little progress is being made and it is only too easy to be discouraged. Sharing of feelings with the knowledge that progress often comes in spurts and after a fallow period can bring comfort to both.

The sharing of positive feelings of warmth and enjoyment of the child may be even more important. Success and achievement, however small, are even more previous when so much effort has gone into helping the child to take even a very small step forward in development. The sharing of a sense of satisfaction and joy that the effort has been worthwhile is of inestimable value to the child, to the parents and to the parent-professional bond.

But such a two way process of support is only possible on the basis of a genuine two way flow of communication and some element of joint undertakings and activities.

4. *Sharing the process of decision making.* Parents have not always played an active part in the process of assessment, planning and decision making. The initiative has lain largely with professionals who may only have informed parents of the outcome or provided them with an opportunity to agree or disagree. But parents have increasingly asserted their wish to be consulted and their right to be more involved is now reflected in legislation.

The most obvious areas for joint decision concern the nature, type and degree of collaboration between parents and professionals. This involves discussion of methods of communication - telephone, written form, notebooks or visits either in school or to the home; frequency of contact, parents' interests in different aspects of the life of the school; the practicalities of time and family commitments. It involves discussion of parents' special skills and interests which they might be encouraged to share with children staff and other parents. They will have valuable and constructive suggestions to make and will in any case enjoy being asked.

Professionals can usefully ask parents actively and directly about their preferences for collaboration. They may need to do so at regular intervals, as circumstances and needs change. They must also accept parents' wishes to opt out and not be involved in detailed programmes of teaching.

5. *Recognition of the individuality of families and the uniqueness of the handicapped child*. Many recipients of professional services have complained bitterly about the generalised judgements of professionals. Obvious examples include the concepts of guilt and over-protection on the one hand and rejection on the other; that a handicapped child means a handicapped family and that all parents must be helped to 'accept' that their child is handicapped. These generalisations and stereotypes need to be constantly questioned; if professionals want to establish comfortable and productive relationships with parents, they will need to explore with each family afresh what the situation means to them and how each family can 'learn to live with' the handicapping condition of one member.

Flexibility of approach is fundamental to partnership. If partnership is not working, the onus is first on professionals to ask themselves how they can more effectively meet the needs of parents and how they can discuss problems on an open and equal basis. Partnership between parents and professionals is justified by the needs of the child, the parents and professionals. Each depends on the knowledge, skills and experience of the other if the needs of the child are to be fully met.

NOTES

1. The section entitled 'Parents of Adolescents and Young Adults' was adapted from a paper *Roles and Needs of Parents of Handicapped Adolescents*, by Peter Mittler, Sally Cheseldine and Helen McConachie in response to a commission from the OECD study on The Handicapped Adolescent. We are grateful for permission to make use of this material (see Mittler, Cheseldine and McConachie, 1981, for the full version).

REFERENCES

Bayley, M. (1973) <u>Mental Handicap and Community
    Care</u>. London: Routledge and Kegan Paul
Boucher, J. (1981) Parents as partners. Talk to DES
    course 'Applications of Warnock', University of
    Manchester, November 1981
Cheseldine, S. and Jeffree, D. (1982) Mentally
    handicapped adolescents: A survey of abilities.
    <u>Special Education: Forward Trends</u> (research
    supplement), <u>9</u>, 19-23
Cook, D. (1980) <u>Walter</u>. London: Penguin Books
Cunningham, C. and Sloper, P. (1977) Parents of
    Down's syndrome babies: their early needs.
    <u>Child: Care, Health and Development</u>, <u>3</u>, 325-347
Cunningham, C. and Sloper, P. (1978) <u>Helping Your
    Handicapped Baby</u>. London: Souvenir Press
Department of Education and Science (1981) <u>Stat-
    istics of Education</u> (1979) Vol. 1: Schools.
    London: HMSO
Hewett, S. (1970) <u>The Family and the Handicapped
    Child</u>. London: Allen and Unwin
International League of Societies for Persons with
    Mental Handicap (1978) <u>Step by Step</u>: <u>Implemen-
    tation of the Rights of Mentally Handicapped
    Persons</u>. Vienna: Lebenshilfe and ILSMH
Jeffree, D. (1980) Personal communication
Mittler, H. (1982) Collaboration between parents
    and special schools: a local survey. Paper
    given to Division of Educational and Child
    Psychology, University of York, January 1982
Mittler, P. (1979) Parents as partners in the edu-
    cation of their handicapped children. Paper
    commissioned by UNESCO, ED/79/conf. 606/7
    Paris: UNESCO
Mittler, P., Cheseldine, S. and McConachie, H.
    (1981) <u>Roles and Needs of Parents of Handi-
    capped Adolescents</u>. Paris: Organisation for
    Economic Cooperation and Development (CERI)
O'Dell, S. (1974) Training parents in behavior
    modification: a review. <u>Psychological Bull-
    etin</u>, <u>81</u>, 418-433
Pugh, G. (1981) <u>Parents as Partners: Intervention
    Schemes and Group Work with Families of Handi-
    capped Children</u>. London: National Children's
    Bureau
Revill, S. and Blunden, R. (1980) <u>A Manual for Imp-
    lementing a Portage Home Training Service for
    Developmentally Handicapped Preschool Children</u>.
    Windsor, Berks.: National Foundation for Edu-
    cational Research

Schafer, N. (1979) <u>Does She Know She's There</u>?
     London: Futura
Spain, B. and Wigley, G. (eds.) (1975) <u>Right from</u>
     <u>the Start: Services for the Preschool Mentally</u>
     <u>Handicapped Child</u>. London: MENCAP
Turnbull, A.P. and Turnbull, H.R. (1982) Parent in-
     volvement in the education of handicapped
     children: a critique. <u>Mental Retardation</u>, <u>20</u>,
     115-122
Whelan, E. and Speake, B. (1979) <u>Learning to Cope</u>.
     London: Souvenir Press
Wilkin, D. (1979) <u>Caring for the Mentally Handi-</u>
     <u>capped Child</u>. London: Croom Helm

SECTION TWO: MEETING PARENTS' NEEDS

Chapter 2

THE PARENTS' PERSPECTIVE OF FAMILY NEEDS AND HOW TO MEET THEM

Philippa Russell

THE NEW PARTNERSHIP

In the course of the last decade, many studies have been published about the needs of children and their families. Families of handicapped children have been the focus of three major British government reports (DHSS, 1976; 1979; DES, 1978) of increasing numbers of research studies and policy statements and of countless professional workers in the statutory and voluntary services.

In many respects, families do receive more help than they used to. Not only have DHSS benefits and the Family Fund (Joseph Rowntree Trust) provided practical help, but increasing awareness of the needs of families and of the value of parental involvement in professional programmes has led to a new dialogue. But it is also possible that the reinforcement of parental confidence and competence may be threatening to some professionals. The new philosophy of shared care carries responsibilities; it also confers benefits and new strengths. The emphasis on support from professionals to parents confirms the Court Report's conclusion that, "We have found no better way to raise a child than to reinforce the abilities of his parents to do so".

But this philosophy also imposes fresh challenges on professionals and may require new initiatives in working with families of handicapped children. For despite the initiatives of the last ten years, the birth of a handicapped child still constitutes a family crisis and calls for complex services for both child and parents. Additionally, the move to 'normalisation' and 'integration', focussing quite properly on the needs of the mentally handicapped as people with rights, can impose heavy new responsibilities on parents whose dual

roles as caretakers and enablers may at times be
confusing and contradictory.

PARENTS' NEEDS

The movement towards early intervention programmes
for young mentally handicapped children has perhaps
distracted some professional awareness from the
fundamental, problematic, and even destructive
personal problems which can accompany any disability
in the family. Partnership with parents pre-
supposes mutual professional and parental adaptation
to the child's disability (as well as an optimistic
and realistic appraisal of capacity for future
development). Unfortunately some parents are
initially themselves too stressed to be able to work
effectively with their own children, so that support
and counselling may be critical to the future
success of any programme.
    It is no accident that pregnant women are said
to be 'expectant': they are expectant of a healthy
normal baby who will fulfil at least some of their
hopes for future family life. If the child is
handicapped, there may be a great gulf between the
dream and the reality. Many parents cannot handle
the initial trauma and may go through a period of
aggressive and irrational behaviour. Cunningham
(1979a) described this aptly as "a model of psychic
crisis at the disclosure of handicap", and noted
that if parents did not receive adequate professional support in this critical period then the shock
reaction could be perpetuated through many months
or even years. (See Chapter 5, this volume.) On
the other hand, the provision of appropriate information, counselling and active involvement in the
care of the child could lead to adaptation and
orientation. It should be added that, whilst many
parents are optimistically told to 'accept' their
handicapped child, few can do so except in a fatal-
istic and usually unproductive way. Whilst the
child may indeed be accepted, few parents will accept
a *disability* and a constructive emphasis on adaptation
and orientation is more productive and realistic.
    Recent developments in services, including home
teaching and home visiting programmes (Pugh, 1981)
and family support centres (Pugh and Russell, 1976)
have demonstrated how these early needs may be met.
The availability of services is also important
since many families may conceal distress and ambivalence beneath a superficial shell of competence.
Brimblecombe (1976) and others have well documented

the widely expressed parental needs for accurate
information, practical help and positive guidance on
how to help their child. But because services for
families with handicapped children are often frag-
mented, professionals may be unaware of pressures
from within the family, and of the often differing
expectations of family members.

Studies of the psychological and emotional
impact of a handicapped child on the family have all
tended to emphasise the potentially damaging impact
of such a child on family life. An investigation of
30 families with a Down's syndrome child found that
33 per cent of the mothers suffered from clinical
depression in the first 18 months of their child's
life, and emotional and sexual problems were common
amongst both mothers and fathers (Gath, 1978).
Wilkin (1979) found that 72 per cent of the mothers
in his study reported problems with 'mental health'
and noted the sense of isolation experienced by many
families, 90 per cent having no free time at all at
weekends and most experiencing a reduction in
ordinary social and leisure experience compared to
friends with non-handicapped children.

Similar observations have been made with regard
to an increase in the rate of divorce and separation
after the birth of a baby nursed in a special care
unit (Leiderman, 1976). In this case, as with
handicap, parents also have to face changed expectations and unanticipated immediate role restructuring. Without recognition of the difficulties
implicit in such restructuring, the family unit will
be vulnerable. Similarly there is some evidence
(Leiderman, 1976; Gath, 1978) that parents were *more*
depressed a year after the birth of their handicapped child - which could be related to falling off
of early support services and home visits about this
time reported by Cunningham and Sloper (1977). All
studies clearly demonstrated the importance of
including fathers in any intervention programme and
in recognising depression and anxiety before
starting any programmes with the child.

Although it is commonly said that the clearly
identified stresses found in families with handicapped children are likely to precipitate marital
breakdown and divorce, the evidence is unclear. As
we live in an age of increased divorce rates across
the population as a whole, it is extremely difficult
to differentiate between other existing problems and
those arising from the presence of a handicapped
child. Lansdown (1981) suggested that, whereas the
additional problems of having a handicapped child

could exacerbate existing difficulties in a poor
relationship, the shared concerns might actually
strengthen the marriage in a good relationship. In
any event it is important to question studies which
assume a pathological model of the family when there
is a handicapped child. As Hewett (1970) noted,
"The general tendency to characterise parents of
handicapped children as guilt ridden, anxiety laden,
over protective and rejecting beings is unfortunate.
... Their common characteristics appear much more
to be the need for money, services and information.
Counselling without these latter is of little
value". Whilst it would be unrealistic to minimise
the trauma of disability in the family and the
necessity to restructure some family roles in the
light of the new responsibility, adverse effects
upon families are not inevitable, and may be prevented by appropriate services.

CHANGING NEEDS, CHANGING SERVICES

Parents invariably emphasise the need for *practical*
information, support and advice. Studies by Hewett
(1970), Bayley (1973), Carr (1974), and Wilkin
(1979) have all highlighted the practical day-to-
day problems encountered by families and the need
to develop services to solve them. The same studies
also emphasised the need to provide a flexible continuum of provision, pointing out that whereas all
families of young children will experience management and care tasks which are demanding due to the
children's dependency, such dependency diminishes
over time in 'ordinary' families. In the case of a
handicapped child becoming an adolescent and young
adult, the care and expectations have a different
quality, and the maturation of siblings, together
with the desire of the parents for greater freedom,
may all impose new strains. In such circumstances,
the parents' quality of life and personal relationships will be less dependent upon sympathy and
counselling (though both are important) than upon
active involvement in planning for their child's
future, education in the developmental process and
how to enhance it and practical help to minimise
the inevitable care tasks in the home.
     In the early days, parents may be very demand-
ing of professional time. They will need not only
verbal advice but practical demonstration of skills
by which they can control and help their child. A
report on the Honeylands Home Visiting Programme
(Devon) observed that, "Some parents have been very

slow to accept that they can actually bring about
progress in their child by working with him"
(Rubissow, Jones, Brimblecombe and Morgan, 1979).
The experience of the first year of the project also
suggested that, "Because we have encountered
parents' participation in observation and goal
setting, we have somewhat deliberately created a
tension of expectation in the parents which is
trickier to work in than a customary clinic visit
where the child is removed from the parents' arms
for treatment and then returned".

Helping families to help themselves must take
into account individual family dynamics. Brazelton
(1979) suggested that the success of any intervention programme should be measured not only by the
child's development but by "increased family comfort, decrease in the divorce rate, lower incidence
of behaviour problems in siblings......perhaps by
pretty soft signs but they may be a lot more important as measures of effectiveness of intervention
than is a rise in IQ or increased motor capacity on
the part of the child". Brazelton described working
with the family as the "soft work" and queried how
many professionals were willing and able to relate
their professional demands to family needs.

Some parents, who have been late in accepting
a permanent handicap, may still cherish hopes of a
'cure' so that disappointment and accompanying
depression can occur many months after the child's
birth. Equally, the availability of a multidisciplinary service is only helpful if the family
have their key worker or 'named person' who will
ensure that they do have access to the team and
fully understand the nature of the advice and
recommendations made by it. Helping a parent to
feel more confident in order to become more competent may be difficult. Parents' groups may be an
invaluable way of establishing not only solidarity
but a real recognition that a parent is a person
with difficulties and *not* a failure. With the
nature of families changing - young and isolated
parents in a mobile society facing particular
problems in developing appropriate parenting skills
- such groups are an obvious way of creating a network of carers for vulnerable families. Also they
may enable parents to admit to hostile or aggressive feelings which are often a normal early reaction
to the discovery of a handicapping condition but
which will be superseded by more positive feeling if
information and support are provided.

Handicap is usually a chronic condition which

will last for the child's whole life. During this
time, parents will themselves change, and so will
their needs. Behaviour problems and physical
burdens of care which are acceptable in a baby or
toddler may become disastrous when the child is a
young adult. Equally, parents have been encouraged
to work with their handicapped child, to have higher
aspirations and, indeed, to expect quality services
as of right. When the handicapped child becomes
the handicapped school leaver, there is likely to
be a conflict between the anticipated and the actual
level of service. Similarly, families will age and
their life styles may alter. Professionals must be
ready to provide a continuum of service which can
meet these changing needs. Many families will
experience critical periods of care when a high
level of intervention is required.

PARENTS AS EDUCATORS

The new move towards the perception of parents as
co-workers and educators has important implications
not only for parents' self image but for their
child's progress and maturation. Newson (1976)
commented when considering parents as a resource in
diagnosis and assessment that:

> We should start from the basic assumption that
> parents in fact have information to impart;
> that parents are experts on their own
> children. This is not to say that they know
> of their children in any systematic or inte-
> grated form; one cannot ask the parents to
> bring along......an ordered case history of
> the child....but the fact that their knowledge
> may be diffuse and unstructured does not
> matter as long as it is available. It is the
> professional's job to make it available.
> Structuring can come later.

Beginning in the USA in the 1950's and 60's,
the development of early intervention and home
teaching programmes has offered major initiatives
in helping parents work with professionals in a
structured way. The idea of a constructive
partnership utilising a systematic teaching
approach makes sound common sense for parents.
Hopefully linked to a system of 'shared care' such
as that offered at Honeylands or the KIDS Family
Centre (Russell, 1981), home teaching programmes
give parents skill to utilise that expertise

recognised by Newson but often dissipated or wasted without appropriate professional support. Since handicap is not an anticipated family disaster (unlike old age, illness or redundancy) parents will be required to develop new skills precisely at the chronological time when they are most vulnerable and confused. Whilst the Honeylands Home Visiting Programme clearly indicated that parents' general needs must be recognised first before they can most effectively carry out home teaching, the great value of early parental involvement programmes lies in the assumption that parents can not only merely monitor the development of their child but that they can also share in goal setting and in devising the means to achieve these goals.

Early intervention programmes teach success. They provide ongoing contact with an involved and informed professional and they are largely *home based*. Whilst there are problems for some professionals in working on a domiciliary basis - Sandow and Clarke (1978) describe in their Hull programme the diffi- culties in working in a small room "surrounded by three generations of a mutually hostile family, in an atmosphere composed of equal parts cigarette smoke, sweat and old chip papers" - the home is where the child spends a large part of the time, and the nature and quality of the home environment will affect that child's development. The balance of any home intervention programme can be determined by what is possible within a particular family and the level of commitment can be matched to what is actu- ally feasible. Additionally, the practical needs of the family can be observed. Washing machines or tumble driers purchased through the Family Fund may be critical to the success of any programme, if they can give the mother *time*. Places for siblings in play groups or other pre-school facilities; advice on practical aids and adaptations; transport for hospital or other clinical visits may all reduce pressure on time and remove additional stress. Since most of us who are parents wish to appear com- petent, it may take the objective eye of a profess- ional to observe what the practical needs really are and to seek to alleviate them. Similarly, parents can talk to a regular professional on sensitive personal areas which they might hesitate to share with a 'one-off' team visit or a busy hospital doctor.

Early intervention programmes tend to fall into two main categories. Parent Workshops (using scarce professional skills very effectively but perhaps making strenuous demands upon some parents) and Home Teaching Programmes all have the common denominator of helping parents help their child. Behavioural techniques were initially used to help children with abnormal behaviour but the same principles were soon applied to children with mental handicap. Behavioural techniques may work in a variety of ways, not only by directly modifying unacceptable behaviour but by teaching new skills which obviate the necessity for the undesirable behaviour. As Cunningham (1975) pointed out, the priorities for parents of mentally handicapped children are not necessarily the same as those for parents of behaviour disturbed children, since the former are more concerned with long-term objectives and sustained treatment and cannot be assured that after 'treatment' their problems will go away. However, the behavioural approach can work extremely well if a suitable detailed programme is developed with long-term support from professionals and clear-cut objectives for the parents to work towards.

Teaching methods vary between the different schemes and the tightness of structure must vary according to the group teaching situation of a workshop or the one-to-one of a programme in the home. The main objective of such programmes for parents is the creation of an environment in which learning can take place. The 'cook book' approach will seldom work, for parents need to understand the principles and concepts of the approaches so that they can in turn intuitively use the skills which they are acquiring. As one psychologist put it to a parent workshop, what happens out of the teaching situation is as important for parents as what happens in it. In any event, any good intervention programme must teach parents to succeed. If the child is severely handicapped and gains will be slow and painful, then the parents will need support. Short-term and long-term goals are critical and the development of developmental checklists such as the Portage Guide and the Parent Involvement Project's charts can enable parents to understand how to break tasks down into basic stages (Bluma, Shearer, Frohman and Hilliard, 1976; Jeffree and McConkey, 1976).

The majority of home intervention projects

involve weekly visits by a home visitor (who may be drawn from a range of disciplines or even a trained volunteer) backed up by a team of professionals. The purpose of the visits is to develop a tailor-made programme with the parents to use in their own home and to place such programmes in the context of a wider spectrum of help and advice from community services. Some other approaches have, however, also been developed. The Honeylands Home Visiting Programme uses home visitors as soon as any child in the catchment area is identified as having a developmental problem. In these very early days, the home visitor is likely to offer family-centred rather than child-centred support, although the two are closely related. Such services, working right from the start, have as a primary objective the alleviation of family stress and the establishment of good and positive relationships with available services. The Haringey 'FISH' Project involved social workers, using a behavioural approach, to work more specifically with the problems of having a mentally handicapped person in the family, including problem-solving through simple programmes and behavioural methods (Kiernan, 1982). Since social workers are sometimes criticised for their 'tea and sympathy' approach - usually a misunderstanding of the nature of social work involvement - the behavioural approach offers a new and more constructive approach to social work in families with a handicapped child. But, whilst making social work more acceptable to the parents, it also makes new demands upon social workers who may be generic in training and have to master new skills in order to be effective.

The parent workshop approach can also be highly successful with parents and, when based on a school, can be a powerful agent for linking objectives between parents and teachers (Pugh, 1981; see Chapter 10, this volume). There has been a suggestion that the workshop approach may succeed better with more articulate parents who can utilise the limited time most effectively. However, Cunningham (1979b) noted that, "The socio-economic and educational level of the parent is not generally correlated with their ability to learn and apply techniques for training and stimulating their child". Workshops like the Kith and Kids 'Two to One' (using volunteers under psychologists' supervision to work with handicapped children over a period of two weeks) very effectively demonstrate that anybody can work well with handicapped children pro-

provided the professional support is good and the
objectives clear (Collins and Collins, 1975). The
Wessex Portage Project also showed that anyone from
a professional or voluntary agency could be trained
in the skills required and methods used by the home
teacher, although - as with any job - certain background experiences will be advantageous (Smith,
Kushlick and Glossop, 1977; Pugh, 1981). As the
Honeylands Home Visiting Programme also found,
because tact, sympathy, care as well as positive
thinking are all necessary when working with vulnerable families, some home teachers (or workshop
organisers) will be better than others.

Potential difficulties
The concept of the 'difficult' or 'hard to reach'
parent is widely perpetuated. But, from the parents' point of view, many so-called maladaptive
responses to having a handicapped child are almost
inevitable in view of the problems faced and the
frequent lack of cohesion in bringing services together. Genuine barriers to progress may lie not
only in early bad experiences (in which parents may
have inadvertently reinforced bad behaviour patterns
in their child) but in some cases with the parents'
loss of confidence in themselves. Parents who perceive themselves as inadequate may be demanding of
professional time and may also be highly dependent
on the 'good professional'. Such parents may literally ask their paediatrician if their child can
watch television or play with certain toys in a
frantic effort to do the right thing. Such parents
desperately need consistent help and guidance; to
be successful a home intervention programme must be
tactfully structured to restore their damaged self-
image and identify their strengths. Additionally,
it should be remembered that because handicap
affects whole families as well as parents, home
intervention should take account of extended family
members and their often contradictory and firmly
held views on how the handicapped child should be
handled.

PARENTS' GROUPS

The development of voluntary organisations has led
to important initiatives in enabling parents to help
themselves - and each other. A well-run and sensi-
tively directed group can do much to reduce stress
and it can also provide the peer group which so
many parents desperately lack when their child is

handicapped. Parents' groups are not necessarily
the same as voluntary organisations, since some
specialist groups, like those established at Health
Service Child Development Units, may meet the needs
of specific groups of parents utilising the same
services at a particular time. Some groups, like
the Southend Scheme (Pugh and Russell, 1977), link
professional and parental help from the earliest
diagnosis and provide not only instant visits and
counselling but introduction into a group of similar
parents. Some like Contact a Family aim to involve
all family members and develop group dynamics to
suit the locality and the parents involved. Again,
many national organisations like MENCAP have a network of local groups which can provide a variety of
parent resources. The importance of the parent
group lies in the increased comfort, solidarity,
practical advice and general support which it can
offer. Many parents of handicapped children are
isolated and lonely. Groups - like Kith and Kids -
can also help them identify their own needs and
literally begin to plan and to influence local
service developments in a positive and informed way.
However, parent groups can only help those who find
them and professionals need to be sensitive to the
local 'grapevine' and ensure that the shy or isolated parent is not missed out.

FIT FOR THE FUTURE? - THE NEW PARTNERSHIP IN ACTION

The concept of parents as partners is gaining
credence. However, such a philosophy of shared care
and active partnership poses a number of difficulties in implementation. The fundamental problem
lies in the creation of a genuine dialogue between
the professional agency and the family. Professionals may find themselves threatened by the
necessary blurring of accepted professional identities. Parents, anxiously seeking diagnosis, may by
implication expect cure and have unrealistically
high expectations of any programmes. Similarly,
some families may be difficult to work with. The
environment may be unsatisfactory, the parents dis-
tressed and oppressed by poor housing, marital
stress or other factors not directly related to the
presenting problem of handicap. Parents may also
expect immediate results. If early success is
achieved, but the child's development then levels
out, the parents may feel that they are to blame for
the delay. If they were able to facilitate early
success, they may feel by implication blamed for any

later failure. Alternatively, some parents will demonstrate exceptional skills in working with their child. Such progress may unconsciously threaten the teacher or professional. In difficult circumstances, it may also be tempting for the professional to overstep the mark and become a 'friend'. But criticism may be unacceptable from a friend and the professional relationship may be threatened and distorted.

Such dilemmas are not insoluble. They are, indeed, hallmarks of success in a system which is flexible to individual needs and where professionals will continually reappraise their method of work. In the end, the relationship between parents and professionals must be enriched by closer co-operation. The acceptance of the philosophy of parental involvement is seldom openly questioned; but the nature of the partnership is one which needs further debate and which must, indeed, reflect the very individual needs and abilities of parents and professionals within the context of their local services.

REFERENCES

Bayley, M. (1973) <u>Mental Handicap and Community Care</u>. London: Routledge and Kegan Paul

Bluma, S., Shearer, M., Frohman, A. and Hilliard, J. (1976) <u>Portage Guide to Early Education</u>. Windsor, Berks: NFER

Brazelton, T. (1970) Case finding, screening, diagnosis and tracking: discussant's comments. In T. Tjossem (ed.) <u>Intervention Strategies for High Risk Infants and Young Children</u>. Baltimore: University Park Press

Brimblecombe, F. (1976) Paediatricians and parents as partners. In <u>The Early Management of Handicapping Disorders</u>. Amsterdam: Associated Scientific Publishers

Carr, J. (1974) The effect of the severely subnormal on their families. In A.M. Clarke and A.D.B. Clarke (eds.) <u>Mental Deficiency: The Changing Outlook</u>, 3rd edition. London: Methuen

Collins, M. and Collins, D. (1976) <u>Kith and Kids</u>. London: Souvenir Press

Cunningham, C. (1975) Parents as therapists and educators. In C.C. Kiernan and F.P. Woodford (eds.) <u>Behaviour Modification with the Severely Retarded</u>. Study Group 8, IRMMH. Amsterdam: Associated Scientific Publishers

Cunningham, C. (1979a) Parent counselling. In M.

Craft (ed.) <u>Tredgold's Mental Retardation</u>, 12th
    edition. London: Ballière Tindall
Cunningham, C. (1979b) Early stimulation of the
    mentally handicapped child. In M. Craft (ed.)
    <u>Tredgold's Mental Retardation</u>, 12th edition.
    London: Ballière Tindall
Cunningham, C. and Sloper, P. (1977) Down's
    syndrome infants: a positive approach to parent
    and professional collaboration. <u>Health
    Visitor</u>, <u>50</u> (2), 32-37
Department of Education and Science (1978) <u>Special
    Educational Needs</u>. Report of the Warnock Comm-
    ittee of Enquiry into the Education of Handi-
    capped Children and Young People. Cmnd 7212.
    London: HMSO
Department of Health and Social Security (1976) <u>Fit
    for the Future</u>. Report of the Court Committee
    of Enquiry into Child Health Services. Cmnd
    6684. London: HMSO
Department of Health and Social Security (1979)
    <u>Report of the Jay Committee of Enquiry into
    Mental Handicap Nursing and Care</u>. Cmnd 7468.
    London: HMSO
Gath, A. (1978) <u>Down's Syndrome and the Family</u>.
    London: Academic Press
Hewett, S. (1970) <u>The Family and the Handicapped
    Child</u>. London: Allen and Unwin
Jeffree, D.M. and McConkey, R. (1976) <u>P.I.P.
    Developmental Charts</u>. Sevenoaks, Kent: Hodder
    and Stoughton
Kiernan, C.C. (1982) <u>Family Involvement with
    Services in Haringey</u>. Final Report to DHSS.
    London: Thomas Coram Research Unit, Institute
    of Education
Lansdown, R. (1981) <u>More than Sympathy</u>. London:
    Tavistock Press
Leiderman, P.H. (1974) Mother at risk. In E.J.
    Anthony and C. Koupernick (eds.) <u>The Child in
    His Family</u>. New York: Wiley
Newson, E. (1976) Parents as a resource in diag-
    nosis and assessment. In <u>The Early Management
    of Handicapping Disorders</u>. Amsterdam:
    Associated Scientific Publishers
Pugh, G. (1981) <u>Parents as Partners</u>. London:
    National Children's Bureau
Pugh, G. and Russell, P. (1976) <u>Shared Care: Support
    for Families with Handicapped Children</u>.
    London: National Children's Bureau
Rubissow, J., Jones, J., Brimblecombe, F. and
    Morgan, D. (1979) Handicapped children and
    their families: their use of available serv-

ices and their unmet needs. In Mixed Communi
cations: Problems and Progress in Medical Care,
No. 12 Nuffield Provincial Hospitals Trust.
London: Oxford University Press

Russell, P. (1981) KIDS - a family support centre.
Concern (National Children's Bureau), no. 38
(Winter 1980/81)

Sandow, S. and Clarke, A.D.B. (1978) Home intervention with parents of severely subnormal
children: an interim report. Child: Care,
Health and Development, 4, 29-39

Smith, J., Kushlick, A. and Glossop, C. (1977) The
Wessex Portage Project: A home teaching service
for families with a pre-school mentally handicapped child. Winchester: Health Care Evaluation Research Team

Wilkin, D. (1979) Caring for the Mentally Handicapped Child. London: Croom Helm

DISCUSSION

In introducing the discussion of her paper, Philippa
Russell again stressed the diversity of needs in
families of mentally handicapped people. Coming to
terms with a child's handicap will proceed at different rates for different family members, and grandparents, for example, often exert a considerable
influence, which may not be considered sufficiently
by professionals.

Secondly, she made the point that, although
professionals should certainly try to make parents
feel competent in the education of their child,
they should beware of thinking of parents as 'professional parents'. If they do, parents may well
feel that it is their responsibility, or in their
power, to develop their child's abilities at a
constant and high rate. Such expectations are
bound to give rise to disappointment and feelings
of failure. Professionals need to help parents to
be both optimistic and realistic, and to allow
parents just to be parents.

Finally, Philippa Russell pointed out that co-
operation between parents and professionals may be
very threatening to professionals. The reasons why
partnership may not be achieved need to be explored - the possibly conflicting views of parents,
professionals and children are a complicated field.

In general discussion, the main topic was
'non-motivated parents', ie. parents who do not
join parents' groups and associations and who de-
cline cooperation with professionals. Labelling of

this type was argued against forcefully by several participants, who pointed out that parents will have good reasons for not joining in. For example, they may have serious personal problems (which are not necessarily connected with the child's handicap), or both parents may be employed, and have large family commitments. They may not get what they want from the service offered and the professionals may not have considered basic necessities such as transport and child-minding. The parents may have real misunderstandings about the handicap; for example, they may see assessment as the child failing a test, after which nothing can be done. Or they may feel strongly that they want to be part of 'normal' society. It was pointed out that in seeking to 'normalize' the children, we expect the parents to be different, ie. collaborating in special programmes, etc. Parents may want a service which enables them to get on with leading their own lives, and also to keep their child.

The other side of the problem is that parents who do join in may be reacting to felt pressure, and avoiding being labelled as 'problems' of one kind or another. Professionals still tend to set up services without adequately consulting parents as to what would make most sense and be of greatest benefit to them.

Chapter 3

MEETING PARENTS' NEEDS: THE ROLE OF THE VOLUNTARY
ORGANISATION

James Ross

There is a strong tradition of 'voluntary' effort in
Britain. Ministers of successive governments have
acknowledged the enormous contribution which the
voluntary agencies make within the total provision
of services. Pioneer workers, such as Dr. Barnardo
and Lord Shaftesbury who rescued unwanted and
neglected children from the streets of London and
other cities more than a century ago, laid foundations in Britain and in other countries for the
health, education and social services which have
developed so rapidly over the last three decades.
But men and women of vision have frequently been
ridiculed for relentlessly defending the needs of
the socially, physically or mentally handicapped.
Even in the 1980's society continues to disregard
certain minority groups and areas of need.

CURRENT ROLES AND RESPONSIBILITIES

The roles and responsibilities of the voluntary
agencies today fall into four main categories:

    . to recognise special needs in our society;
    . to pioneer services by a process of research
      and example;
    . to present to government the established facts
      which clearly define the problems and the
      needs;
    . to lobby for public and government recognition
      of the responsibility to provide services.

In terms of the first role, there are those who
argue that the increase in statutory provision for
those in need of special services is diminishing the
responsibilities of the voluntary movement. In fact
the opposite is the case. Growth in the standard

of living and the enormous development of scientific and technical skills have created a materialistically rich and complicated society. Such progress has presented increasingly difficult problems of expectations and standards. Voluntary organisations are an essential part of a monitoring process which alerts the social conscience to the casualties of change and development; voluntary organisations identify the responsibilities of society. For example, they stimulated the debate about the response of government to the suffering of drug-damaged children and their families.

Secondly, voluntary agencies establish services as a temporary measure to relieve suffering and deprivation as far as possible. One advantage of a voluntary agency is its independence, which allows for a quick response and direct appeals for support. An essential part of this process is research: the collection, examination and exploration of the essential components of the problem. The widest implications of meeting special needs must be properly analysed for a meaningful programme to be developed.

Thirdly, it is the voluntary organisations' responsibility to represent people's needs by a clear identification of the facts. The processes of identification and collation of information are slow and demanding because those with the most serious problems are scattered in the community. They may not know of the existence of others in a similar position, nor of the organisations who may be able to help. They are frequently isolated by the problems. It is not hard to recognise, for example, the enormous difficulties of the families who struggle to look after a severely multiply handicapped child or adult at home, but it is extremely difficult to establish and assess the total problem. Neither the voluntary organisations nor central government really knows the extent of the needs.

For example, there are few really good examples of special care provision in special schools or Adult Training Centres, not because teachers do not care or are not convinced that more effort would be beneficial but because we are not sure what to do. Much more research is needed into methods of education and stimulation of profoundly retarded multiply handicapped people. One role of the voluntary agencies is to ensure that they are fairly represented in the claims upon national and local resources in providing for such needs.

63

Fourthly, a determined and articulate campaign is organised to influence the policy and programmes of government. The British democratic system depends to a large extent on lobbying by 'pressure groups'. The process is rarely sensational: policy is ultimately determined by consultation, working parties, evidence to Government Committees and Royal Commissions, and more often than not through the interest of a Member of Parliament who is able to gain the support of colleagues.

In recent years, voluntary organisations have had an increasing burden of campaigning to have legislation implemented: people in need are frequently not receiving services to which they are already legally entitled. Campaigning for the implementation of rights is one of the most disturbing responsibilities of the voluntary agencies today.

MENCAP

The Royal Society for Mentally Handicapped Children and Adults (MENCAP) has 40,000 members in 500 local societies served by 12 Regional Offices. It is a registered charity, supported largely by voluntary contributions. The primary objective of the Society is to secure for mentally handicapped people provision commensurate with their needs. To this end, the Society aims to increase public knowledge and awareness of the problems faced by mentally handicapped people and their families, and thus to create a sympathetic climate of public opinion as a necessary prerequisite of their acceptance into the community. Provision includes:

- support and help for the parents of mentally handicapped people through a network of Local Societies and Regional Offices in all parts of the country;
- funds and support for research into various aspects of mental handicap;
- books and literature, and the quarterly *Journal of Mental Deficiency Research* for professionals and research workers, and *Parents Voice* for parents and general readers;
- specialist advisory and information services for the lay public and for professional workers on all aspects of mental handicap;
- an ongoing programme to facilitate the sharing of knowledge on all aspects of mental handicap by means of symposia, conferences and information exchange sessions.

The Society developed from groups of parents of
mentally handicapped children meeting together and
supporting each other, trying to relieve both emotional and practical problems. Parents have responded magnificently to the challenges. Finding the
energy after coping all day, and maybe several hours
during the previous night, to turn out for a meeting
to share with others who themselves may also be worn
out by the sheer physical demands of coping with the
everyday chores, takes a lot of determination and
loyalty. One young mother summed it up recently:

> I seem to find new energy from the realisation
> that at last I can talk and relax with other
> parents who know what it is like. Most of the
> time I feel other people don't understand how
> guilty or angry and bitterly disappointed my
> husband and I feel. The people from the Town
> Hall, like the social worker and health
> visitor, don't seem to understand at all. Our
> doctor, when we go to see him seems to be more
> embarrassed than we are. Most of the time we
> have to put on an act of acceptance and it is
> difficult to relax or be natural. I don't
> know what I would do, or that I could cope,
> without the precious few hours once or twice
> a week when I meet other parents at our local
> society.

It may seem hard for some to realise that within the welfare state system many of the fundamental
needs of parents are not and perhaps cannot be met
by medicine, education, psychology or the social
sciences. This is not to say that such expertise
is unimportant, or not needed; but the services cannot stand on their own. Parents have proved from
long and bitter experience that the parent-to-parent
service of their local group is vital to the success
of all the other elements which contribute to a responsive and caring service of practical value to
families with a mentally handicapped member.

VOLUNTARY WELFARE VISITORS

In 1974, MENCAP established a Voluntary Welfare
Visitors scheme, with the aim of ensuring that
families have as much information and advice as is
necessary to obtain the best services available in
their area. Each local society selects a team of
parents who are prepared to attend a training course
and also to make a special study of the rights of

mentally handicapped people and their families, in
addition to compiling detailed information about all
the services and facilities available in the local
area which may be of help. The detail of this comprehensive source of reference is vitally important
because the primary function of the Voluntary Welfare Visitor is to direct parents to the right kind
of help and to avoid the unnecessary stress of being
passed from one person or department to another.
The Voluntary Welfare Visitor supplies the names of
the professionals responsible for providing the
service and often accompanies the parents, if they
so wish, on their initial enquiries. The main
advantage is that parents in each local society know
they have another parent to whom they can turn for
help and advice - a parent who has been selected and
who has agreed to make his or her contribution to
the self-help group as a 'specialist' in advice,
support and direction. The Voluntary Welfare
Visitor is a 'direction indicator' rather than a
provider of services.

A second function of the Voluntary Welfare
Visitor is to give moral support to parents, to give
them the assurance that they are not alone, isolated
or forgotten. This caring relationship is offered
to families whether or not they are members of the
local Society. Thirdly, there may be need for
immediate practical help. This can range from
advising a parent on how to complete an application
for the Attendance Allowance to urgent problems
where no other sources of help can be found at the
time. For example, a Welfare Visitor may need to
find immediate overnight accommodation for a mentally handicapped child or financial assistance from
the local society welfare funds.

The Voluntary Welfare Visitor must foster a
good working relationship with the various statutory
and voluntary agencies. For example, some have
established regular informal meetings with health
visitors and social workers, by a monthly coffee
morning or through a mother and baby group, when the
professional workers are invited to call in for a
short time. It is not unusual to find health and
social services referring parents to MENCAP's
Voluntary Welfare Visitors; the expertise of the
parent visitor is increasingly being recognised by
professionals.

All Voluntary Welfare Visitors are required to
follow a 'code of practice' which has been compiled
by MENCAP to help them in their work and also to
avoid any misunderstanding about their role. It

covers difficult areas such as confidentiality, areas of possible conflict with the statutory services, welfare funds, and reports.

The following guidelines show in greater detail how the MENCAP Voluntary Welfare Service operates.

1. The most important work of a Local Society is to be a good source of advice and help for parents of mentally handicapped people. The Local Society must be aware of the needs of its members and it is essential to ensure a well organised Welfare and Advisory Service is given the highest priority.

2. Each Local Society should have at least one Voluntary Welfare Visitor. According to the size of membership and the geographical area to be covered, it is often desirable to have a small team of such Visitors.

3. The Voluntary Welfare Visitor (VWV) is in a key position in the self-help philosophy of the Local Society. It is an important office which requires careful consideration by those responsible for the appointment. Obviously it is a position of trust and members must be able to share their problems or difficulties in complete confidence with the person or persons selected. The VWV may be recruited from the membership of the Local Society, or alternatively a suitable person or persons from elsewhere in the community may be invited to undertake this vital role. If it is necessary to appoint more than one VWV, it is important to designate one of them as responsible for co-ordinating the work and also for being responsible to the Executive Committee of the Local Society, as well as to liaise with the Regional Office when professional help and guidance is required from the Royal Society.

4. The VWV is an official (the same as the Chairperson, Secretary, Nominee member, Treasurer, etc) of the Local Society and must be accountable to the Local Society Executive Committee. Local Societies are advised to have a separate Welfare and Advisory Sub-Committee, and a Welfare Fund should be established to meet the out of pocket expenses of the VWV (e.g., training courses, conferences, reference books, travel, postage, telephone and stationery) and any exceptional needs of families which

cannot be met by statutory funding.

5. The role of the VWV is to give immediate
   help and support to parents who are in need,
   and to assure parents they are not alone,
   isolated or forgotten. The main concern
   should be to develop a caring relationship
   and a sympathetic understanding to which
   parents can turn whenever they feel the
   need for moral support, advice or practical
   assistance.

6. The Royal Society provides a full programme
   of support and training for Local Society
   Welfare and Advisory Services. Professional
   support is provided from the Regional
   Offices and VWVs should contact them whenever they require advice. The Directors of
   Regional Services and their staff provide
   the professional support, and the Central
   Office in London is able to give additional
   specialist advice and guidance. Training
   for VWVs is provided by a network of courses
   which are offered on a regular programme in
   London, and as the need arises in the
   regions. Training Courses will usually be
   organised in any part of the country if
   there are ten or more people prepared to
   attend.

7. The Training Courses have been carefully
   planned to meet the basic needs of the wide
   cross-section of VWVs and to help them
   understand the welfare state system, the
   statutory services and the rudiments of the
   legal rights of mentally handicapped
   people - children and adults. The syllabus
   is approved by the Royal Society's National
   Council and leads to official registration
   on the National Register for all VWVs who
   have satisfactorily completed both parts of
   the Training Courses and who continue to
   work by the 'Code of Good Practice' and the
   'Basic Rules' taught as an essential part
   of the course syllabus.

8. It is recommended that all Local Societies
   do everything possible to encourage and make
   it possible for VWVs to attend the Training
   Courses. The Department of Health and
   Social Security and local authorities recognise the importance of the professional
   support and the training courses provided
   by the Royal Society. The credibility of
   this nationwide Welfare and Advisory Service

depends upon the maintenance of the highest
possible standards and it is therefore essential to ensure Local Societies affiliated
to the Royal Society are trained according
to the National Syllabus of Training
approved by the National Council. Only VWVs
who have completed the National Syllabus of
Training can be officially recognised and
placed on the National Register.

TRAINING AND SUPPORT OF VOLUNTARY WELFARE VISITORS

By 1981, there were 1500 Voluntary Welfare Visitors
working in the local societies. Each had attended
a comprehensive training programme to give them the
information and guidelines necessary to help other
parents. The training is divided into two courses.
The first covers the basic legal framework for
services, statutory rights, and an analysis of the
service providers. The second course includes the
Social Security system, the range of benefits,
allowances and services available together with a
detailed study of the role of the various professionals (e.g., social workers, health visitors,
teachers, etc.) in supporting mentally handicapped
people and their families.

Outline Syllabus for Part One

1. Introduction	. The national scheme
	. The Welfare Visitor role
	. The Code of Good Practice – "Confidentiality"
2. Family Support	. Advice and information
	. Counselling
	. The Code of Good Practice – "Keeping Records"
3. Important Legislation – session 1	. The Education Acts 1970 and 1981
	. Local Authority Social Services Act 1970
	. The Code of Good Practice – "Demarcation Lines"
4. Important Legislation – session 2	. Chronically Sick and Disabled Persons Act 1970
	. The Mental Health Acts 1959 and 1982

	. The Code of Good Practice - "Authority and Action"
5. The Agencies	. Public and Statutory
	. Voluntary and Charitable
	. The Code of Good Practice - "Welfare Funds"
6. Local Welfare Services	. Family problems
	. Co-operation and Co-ordination
	. The Code of Good Practice - "Accountability and Reports"

Outline Syllabus for Part Two

1. Introduction	. Review of the services
	. The 'key' workers
	. Practical help series - The Local Society
2. Domiciliary Support	. The Health Visitor
	. The Social Worker
	. Practical help series - The Regional and National Organisation
3. Social Security	. The Social Security System
	. Social Security Benefits
	. Practical help series - Local guide and information
4. Education and Training	. The School Teacher
	. The Adult Training Centre
	. Practical help series - Leisure, Gateway Clubs, Holidays
5. Residential Care	. In the community
	. In the hospital
	. Practical help series - The Trusteeship Scheme
6. Specialist Advice and Support	. The Therapists
	. The Counselling and Advisory Agencies
	. Practical help series - Training and Employment

Part two of the course is open only to those who have completed part one. Each part of the training course covers six one-and-a-half-hour sessions as a minimum and those attending are requested to follow a basic reading list. The background reading is an important part of the total scheme because it provides information which it is not possible to cover in the formal sessions. In addition to the reading list, some basic reference books are recommended. Some of the sessions include a period of practical exercises to reinforce the instruction. Time is allowed for clarification, questions and discussion.

Regular seminars and meetings are held nationally and in the regions to support Voluntary Welfare Visitors and to provide them with up-to-date information on the development of services and changes in government benefits or policies. A Welfare and Rights Communications Pack, which ensures Visitors are well-informed on all matters concerning mentally handicapped people, is issued three times each year. National and international news, events and projects are included if they are of particular value to the work of Local Societies and parents. It is compiled especially for Voluntary Welfare Visitors but many professionals, local authorities, hospitals, colleges and other bodies find it a valuable reference resource.

CONCLUSION

This chapter has described the roles and responsibilities of voluntary agencies in the context of the present welfare state. One role in particular has been focussed on: the importance of ensuring that the delivery of services to mentally handicapped people and their families matches their entitlement and needs. Roles change as provision of services develops. Helping people to know their rights and what is available, or should be available, may be the major task of the voluntary organisations in the future. Of course, we have a long way to go before it will be the only task; but it is a serious mistake to secure statutory responsibility for services without carefully monitoring their implementation.

DISCUSSION

From discussion it seemed that in all the countries represented at the Seminar voluntary organisations have the same ultimate goal that society should take full responsibility for its handicapped members.

How far the voluntary organisations have travelled towards this goal depends both on the initiatives taken by parents and also on the political and social conditions in each country.

Erica Lund compared the situation in Sweden with that in Britain. She noted that the parallel body to MENCAP has the same number of members, even though Sweden has less than a sixth of the general population of England, Wales and Northern Ireland. (Scotland has a separate voluntary organisation.) The growth of organised parent groups in Sweden has taken place over a period of 25 years. In the beginning, they placed primary importance on gathering funds in order to be able to promote their own activities; professionals such as teachers in special education and psychologists were hired to lead these activities.

During the 1960's and the first half of the 1970's public agencies gradually assumed financial responsibility for various activities which had first been developed by parent groups, for example, nursery schools and summer camps. At the present time, voluntary organisations play an important role as pressure groups; but in terms of care, development and research, the contribution of statutory agencies has become dominant. In order to reach this level, voluntary groups have worked at intestigating needs, proposing improvements, and influencing both public opinion and political interests. The methods adopted reflect how voluntary groups now see their primary role. They go further than simply studying facts and information: through self-education in small groups they try to create conditions in which parents develop pride in being the parent of their handicapped child, and are more able to fulfil the task of providing the best possible social environment for the whole family.

James Ross commented further on the political role of the voluntary organisations, and mentioned that MENCAP now has an office in the House of Commons, where staff members monitor all political debates and can contact Members of Parliament whenever a debate concerns the rights of mentally handicapped people. It seems to be effective in directly influencing political decision-making.

Discussion then focussed on the topic of confidentiality. Parents from several countries expressed dissatisfaction at the lack of open access to files concerning their child. Confidentiality can also be a problem between professionals. For example, some felt that at the present time to open up all records on a child's development could lead to misunderstanding if parents cannot interpret the wording of a letter or a report, or distress if the terminology is cold and clinical. Some professionals have set up two sets of records, one open and one closed, in an attempt to overcome these problems. It was forcefully argued that if a copy of every document written about a child were given to the parents, it would compel professionals to think even more carefully about what they write. Even if the subject of confidentiality were to be regulated by law, the implementation of rules would ultimately depend on the willingness of professionals to allow scrutiny of their own field of practice.

SECTION THREE: INFANCY AND EARLY CHILDHOOD

Chapter 4

INFANT DEVELOPMENT PROGRAMMES IN BRITISH COLUMBIA

Dana Brynelsen

INTRODUCTION

History

The first home-based Infant Development Programme in British Columbia was started by a group of parents of infants with developmental handicaps and professionals involved with services for these children in Vancouver in 1972. With support and funding from the Ministry of Human Resources, the provincial goverment department responsible for funding family support services, Infant programmes were then developed elsewhere in British Columbia. A Provincial Steering Committee was appointed by the Minister of Human Resources in 1975 to set terms of reference for this new service as it expanded through the province.

The terms of reference for the development and operation of Infant Development Programmes were designed to encourage standard practices of service delivery and are described in this chapter. They were developed, however, with consideration for the diverse circumstances of geography, population cluster, climate and availability of specialized resources in rural areas, which characterize this large province. Therefore, in addition to standard practices, there are also significant individual differences among the programmes currently in operation. At present, 28 programmes serve an annual population of approximately 1,500 infants and their families. Since the programme's inception in 1972, more than 4,000 infants and their families have received regular service from Infant Development Programmes.

Rationale

In common with similar services in the U.S.A. and elsewhere in Canada, Infant Development Programmes are based on the following theories:

1. Infancy is an important period of life; delays in development during this period may have long-lasting, cumulative effects on the patterns of development of any child, as well as on the patterns of interaction between the child and the family.
2. Intervention for children with developmental problems will be most effective if begun as early in the child's life as possible.
3. The family unit is the most crucial source of learning, developmental encouragement and emotional support available to the child.

The family thus becomes the primary focus of services for the Infant Development Programme and the home is the centre around which programming is built. While there is no question about the absolute necessity for good diagnostic services, medical treatment, genetic counsellors and other medical, social and educational agents, the focus of this programme is to provide early intervention in the home through and with the parents. The aims of the programme are to help parents make optimal use of available services, to enlarge their knowledge of those factors pertinent to the overall growth and development of their child and to learn skills which will enable them to encourage the development of their child.

Philosophy

The principles of 'normalisation' form the foundation for the development and operation of the Infant Development Programmes. Attempts are made to incorporate these principles at an individual level with families, at a community level with individual programmes and at a provincial level with policy making.

To illustrate this, we might encourage a family with a child who has a handicap to participate in a regular family recreation programme in the community, as opposed to recommending a segregated recreation programme serving only the child with the handicap. At a community level, we would request that the Infant Programme operate from the Public Health Office rather than from a specialized agency that serves only the handicapped. At a provincial level, we have worked with the government in developing community resources as alternatives to instituting resources for the family who has a child with a handicap.

POPULATION SERVED

Infant Development Programmes serve children from birth to three years, at which time they are eligible for pre-school. Children identified as developmentally delayed in one or more major skill areas, children with specific handicapping conditions such as Down's syndrome or physical handicap, and children at risk for delay, such as premature infants with low birth weight, are eligible for service.

A special note of caution must be sounded, however, with regard to involvement of 'at risk', infants in a programme that serves children with handicaps. Infants at risk are defined as that population of infants who experience adverse prenatal, post-natal and/or socio-economic factors that are thought to contribute to developmental handicaps. Inclusion of at risk infants into programmes serving children with diagnosed handicaps must be done carefully. Parental expectations as to the developmental outcome of their infant appear to play an important role with regard to child development. Therefore, anxiety generated by a poor prognosis for development and subsequent referral to a programme serving infants with handicaps can be translated by the parents into lower expectations for normal developmental progress. This may contribute to developmental delay in a potentially normal infant (Kearsley, 1979).

It should also be noted that the programme accepts infants for whom no more appropriate service exists. For example, in large urban areas which have home-based programmes for hearing impaired infants, a hearing impaired infant would not be accepted unless another developmental problem was present. Hearing impaired infants are accepted into Infant Development Programmes in rural areas where more specialized service are not available. Cerebral palsy societies throughout British Columbia sponsor a variety of services for infants and children with cerebral palsy, as well as for children with other handicaps. Therefore, the Infant Development Programme serves very few children with cerebral palsy or other orthopaedic problems, as excellent resources are widely available to serve this population.

Table 4.1 gives a diagnostic breakdown of 738
infants who were receiving service from the Infant
Development Programmes of British Columbia in May,
1981. It should be understood that the table

Table 4.1: Reasons for Infants Entering Infant
Development Programmes

	No. of infants	Per cent of total
Developmental delay (more than one skill area)	208	28
Mental retardation (includes infants with Down's syndrome)	171	23
At risk	118	16
Developmental delay (one skill area)	102	14
Multiple handicaps	54	7
Sensory impairment (vision or hearing)	36	5
Cerebral palsy	25	3
Seizure disorder	12	2
Behaviour problem	12	2
Totals	738	100%

represents, in brief form, a compilation of the
diagnostic information available for each child.
Many children move into other diagnostic categories
as they grow older. Some will cease to be
'labelled' when they catch up to the norm for their
ages and are no longer in need of special services.

Population Trends Over Time
Statistics on 1,000 infants referred to Infant
Development Programmes from 1973 to 1978 were compared to the caseload of May, 1981, and revealed a
positive trend in terms of population served. In
1978, 60 per cent of infants who had received service had diagnosed handicaps and 40 per cent were
developmentally delayed or at risk. Over time, as
the programmes have gained acceptance by the medical
community, other professionals and the public in
general, the referral of infants with developmental
delay or at risk for developmental delay has increased. At this time, 60 per cent of the popu-

lation in Infant Development Programmes is delayed
or at risk and 40 per cent has diagnosed handicaps.
This is encouraging because a significant number of
children who are delayed may benefit from early
intervention and will have a much greater chance of
intensive medical investigation and referral to
appropriate pre-schools if they are involved to
intervention programmes early in life.

Another significant and positive trend is the
age at referral. In the early years of the programme, the average age at referral, both for children with diagnosed handicaps and developmental
delay, was 15 months. In 1981, 50 per cent of infants in Infant Development Programmes were referred
under six months of age; 80 per cent were referred
by 18 months.

REFERRALS TO INFANT DEVELOPMENT PROGRAMMES

To encourage early referrals, Infant Development
Programmes have an open referral policy: parents as
well as professionals may refer to the programme.
An open referral policy, as compared to more traditional referral policies which require a physician's
referral, was established for a number of reasons.

British Columbia does not have universal surveillance of the child population. Generally, a
surveillance system ensures appropriate referral to
social, educational, or medical services at the time
that delay is evidence in an infant. Without such
a system, however, referrals are not the mandated
responsibility of any individual or agency. Therefore, it has been an unfortunate, documented fact
that, in British Columbia, the suspicion of parents
that, "Something is wrong with my child," has sometimes taken up to three years to confirm through
medical diagnosis (Sheps and Robinson, 1979). If
referral to the Infant Programme was dependent on a
physician's confirmation of delay and referral, many
of the early referrals we receive would not occur.

Some parents have described the period between
suspicion of delay, confirmation of concern, and
referral to a programme as being the most difficult
period to cope with emotionally. From our experience, the longer this period continues the more
difficult it is to intervene in effecting change in
parental attitudes and in helping the parents to set
realistic goals for their child's development. One
key to this relates to how the parents perceive
themselves in relation to the child's development.
Studies elsewhere, as well as one study of 59 devel-

opmentally delayed infants in Infant Development
Programmes in this province, demonstrate that, generally, parents providing the optimal home environment were those who believed in their ability to influence their child's development and felt a personal sense of responsibility toward that development (Tolleson, 1978). The parent with prolonged,
unsuccessful caretaking experiences, which may
result from not understanding how best to meet the
baby's needs, may feel unable to influence the
child's development. That parent is at risk for
withdrawing more and more from normal parenting
practices. These pre-diagnostic experiences have
been significant factors in post-diagnostic decisions resulting in out-of-home care for many children in this province (Brynelsen, 1982).

   To prevent further delay in terms of referral
and contact with the family, parental or professional referrals are taken by telephone by Infant
Development Programme staff. Information is collected which includes family history, diagnostic and
assessment information and professionals presently
involved. A home visit by an Infant Development
Programme staff member to the family is scheduled,
generally within two weeks of contact with the programme. Further information about the family, the
infant and the professionals involved is collected
at that time. Services provided by the Infant Development Programme are described and the family is
asked to identify those needs that they feel are
priorities for them (e.g., assistance in feeding)
and practical suggestions that may be of assistance
are made on the initial visit.

Contact with Other Community Professionals and Agencies
Professionals involved with the family are informed
in writing that the family has been referred. These
professionals generally include the family doctor,
paediatrician and public health nurse.[1] They are
encouraged to work closely with the family and
Infant Development Programme staff persons in
sharing relevant information and co-ordinating intervention strategies. However, time constraints
caused by heavy work loads contribute to less than
adequate information sharing and joint planning for
some families. As well, some professionals regard
some children (e.g., severely multiply handicapped
children) as less entitled to their time and efforts
than other children, and are not prepared to work
with other agencies on their behalf. Infant Development Programme staff do send regular six-month

reports on children to professionals involved with
the family. These reports present a developmental
profile, current programme strategies, goals and
recommendations. This reduces the risk of conflicting advice if reciprocity of information sharing is not achieved. Case review committees, comprised of Infant Development Programme staff, a
community physician, public health nurse and physiotherapist consultant, meet regularly to review new
referrals and progress of children on the caseload.
This also provides a medium for collaboration and
coordination of services.

Referral Trends Over Time
When a programme starts in a community, the primary
referral sources are public health nurses, who
generate 80 per cent of referrals. Physician referrals constitute approximately five to ten per
cent and parents five to ten per cent. Programmes
which have operated for more than two years in a
community have referral trends as described in
Table 4.2.

Table 4.2: Referral Trends for Established
Programmes

Referral source	Per cent of pop.
Public health nurses	40
Physician	31
Parent	10
Social services	7
Other agencies	7
Other I.D. Programmes	5
Total	100%

The increase in physician referrals is
attributed to the following factors. Parents are
encouraged to talk to the child's physician about
their involvement in the programme and physicians
receive copies of the six-month reports done by
Infant Development Programme staff on infants. The
physician representative on the Local Advisory
Committee is responsible for educating his or her

colleagues regarding the importance of early diagnosis of developmental delay and early referral to
intervention programmes.

STRUCTURE OF INFANT DEVELOPMENT PROGRAMMES

Funding
All Infant Development Programmes receive 100 per
cent funding from the government. The programme
budgets comprise mainly salaries for Infant Development Programme staff and transportation (mileage)
costs, which include in-service training.

Administration
Infant Development Programmes are sponsored by a
variety of voluntary societies in British Columbia.
These societies include associations for the mentally handicapped, neurological societies and family
and children's services societies. The staff
reports to the executive director or board of the
voluntary society, but receive direction and support
from a Local Advisory Committee to the Infant Development Programme.

Local Advisory Committee
This committee of the board of the sponsoring
society serves as a voluntary (unpaid) multidisciplinary consultant body which gives direction and
support to Infant Development Programme staff.
Membership on each committee must include: parents
of developmentally delayed infants who are receiving
service or who have received service from the Infant
Development Programme; a public health nurse; a
physician; a Ministry of Human Resources social
worker and a physiotherapist. Other professionals,
such as psychologists, speech therapists and early
education specialists, if available in a community,
are encouraged to sit as members.
     The aim of the committee is to concern itself
with the development and continuity of programmes
and services for developmentally delayed infants and
their families in the geographical area covered by
the Infant Development Programme. The terms of reference include the following:

     . to be aware of the standards set by the
       Provincial Steering Committee and the Ministry
       of Human Resources and to assist the Infant
       Development Programme in meeting these stand-
       ards;
     . to provide consultation to the society in the

84

hiring and on-going monitoring of the Infant
Development Programme staff;
. to assist the staff in reaching the goals of
the Infant Development Programme;
. to encourage the development of quality
programmes for infants and to develop proposals
to overcome gaps or inadequacies in service for
developmentally delayed infants;
. to encourage parent-to-parent support;
. to foster good relationships between parents
receiving services and professionals;
. to facilitate the sharing of information in the
area of early intervention.

INFANT DEVELOPMENT PROGRAMME STAFF

Requirements
Staff of local Infant Development Programmes must
have professional training in a field or fields related to early childhood development (e.g. nursing,
therapy, early childhood education). Demonstrated
ability to work with infants and very young children
and their families, as well as other professionals,
is desirable. Organizational ability and the
ability to operate independently are essential.
Individuals considered for the position of
Infant Development Programme worker must subscribe
to the following management principles:

. decisions are centred on the child and the
family;
. family members are the principal decision
makers and advocates for their child;
. a developmental disability may have lifelong
ramifications;
. a transdisciplinary approach is essential.

Infant Development Programmes attempt to utilize
the transdisciplinary approach in service delivery.
"Transdisciplinary describes the ability of professionals to cross over and function effectively in
areas outside their primary specialization," which
facilitates coordination of service (Accardo and
Capute, 1980). It has become increasingly evident
that coordination of services for families who have
children with developmental problems can be as
important as availability of expert consultants. In
fact, lack of coordination of services has resulted
in out-of-home care for a number of children in the
province. Primary involvement of one person is an
essential ingredient in the transdisciplinary model.

The role of the primary person is gathering information from a variety of sources and translating it
into daily, practical use for the family (Bricker,
1976).

Role
The Infant Development Programme worker has a multi-
faceted job in the home-based programme. One major
aspect of the job involves working with the family
to develop an individualized programme for the
infant that will promote development in major skill
areas. To develop an individualized programme, the
worker ensures that:

- . the infant is assessed on a regular basis
  by standardized assessment;
- . input from parents and appropriate consulting
  professionals is actively pursued;
- . resource materials and programmes of instruction relating to normal and atypical development
  are utilized.

Ongoing evaluation of short-term and long-term
goals and methods of attainment are worked out with
the family during the course of home visits, and the
programme is continually revised in consultation
with the family and consulting professionals to meet
the changing development and needs of the infant and
family.
Medical assessment throughout the infant's stay
in the programme is actively sought. At times,
limited resources in some rural areas make it difficult to obtain comprehensive assessment and diagnostic services, but the programme workers are aware
of the importance of sound diagnostic and treatment
procedures. Specialists, such as paediatric physiotherapists or speech therapists, are actively sought
out and referrals are made to these specialists when
available. The active participation of these specialists in planning the individual programme for
each child is encouraged by the staff.
The second major aspect of the job is that the
Infant Development Programme workers must provide
expertise on the resources available in the community for the family and the infant. Staff provide
the parents with information about various programmes, policies and services that may pertain to
the family's needs. In consultation with consulting
professionals, they also help the family learn more
about the handicapping condition. Opportunities are
available, informally or through Pilot Parents, to

meet other families who have a son or daughter with a similar handicap. For some families, this has been the most helpful service provided by the Programme. The Infant Development Programme workers help the family locate and utilize specialized services and information which may enhance their care of the atypical youngster.

Recruitment and maintenance of a qualified and competent staff has been pursued through a number of organizational methods.

1. Societies and Local Advisory Committees establish hiring committees comprised of parents and professionals to screen, select and hire staff and to monitor their performance.
2. Guidelines, job descriptions and relevant criteria to be considered when hiring are described.
3. All new staff members are provided with a practicum placement at the beginning of their employment; evaluations are made during that time and throughout an initial six-month probationary period by the Programme Supervisor, Local Advisory Committee and Provincial Advisor, if requested.

SERVICES PROVIDED BY INFANT DEVELOPMENT PROGRAMMES

All Infant Development Programmes in British Columbia must provide the following services:

1. Home visits will be made on a regular basis by professional staff to assist the family in planning learning activities and to utilize appropriate resources in the community.
2. Parents will be given the opportunity to meet other parents who are successfully coping with the problems of caring for a handicapped child.
3. Parents will be encouraged to attend workshops, lectures and parent meetings which will further their understanding and knowledge of child development.
4. A resource library and toys will be available for loan to the family.
5. The family will be inffrmed of alternatives open to their child as he or she grows older and will be encouraged to take part in any decision making process regarding education

or health services.

Other services may be provided by the Infant Development Programme. These services might include a group situation for infants, out-of-boundary services and providing practicum placements for students.

THE ROLE OF THE PARENT IN INFANT DEVELOPMENT PROGRAMMES

Infant Development Programmes are designed to encourage the participation of parents in the home, in the community and at a provincial level. The open referral system enables parents to initiate contact with this service. Parents work with Infant Development Programme staff in planning activities for their infant. Their priorities and needs and those of their infant, as they perceive them, are incorporated into the home programme.

Initially, parents may be unaware or uncertain as to the importance of their contribution to decisions on management issues made regarding their child. This relates, in part, to traditional parent-professional encounters where the professional instructs or delivers a service to the non-professional who is usually in a passive, receiving position. However, it is the responsibility of Infant Development Programme staff involved to encourage active participation of the parent at whatever level seems appropriate and to whatever degree the parent wishes to be involved.

Beyond the individual work with their infant, parents are involved in planning and/or running workshops for other parents. Parent to parent support groups and individual counselling through Pilot Parents are set up by, or liaise closely with, parents involved in Infant Development Programmes. At the organizational level, parents whose sons or daughters are or were in Infant Development Programmes work with professionals in directing and monitoring the programme in each community. Parents are appointed by the Deputy Minister of Human Resources to sit with other professionals on the Provincial Steering Committee of the Infant Development Programme. At this level, they advise on the implementation and operation of the programmes throughout British Columbia.

CONCLUSIONS

Infant Development Programmes are a relatively new
model of service in British Columbia. Their expans-
ion throughout the province has not occurred without
some struggle or conflict with existing, more traditional services or approaches.

There are a variety of specialized services for
children with developmental problems in British
Columbia. They range from institutions housing up
to 800 children and adults to segregated, special
pre-schools and schools. Efforts have been made by
these agencies to put the principles of normalisation and integration into practice but, in many
instances, change has been slow. Because many
families involved in Infant Development Programmes
require services from these agencies, close working
relationships are important. However, philosophical
differences have caused some conflict in the past.
In addition, Infant Development Programmes have been
criticized for adopting a transdisciplinary
approach; some professionals do not subscribe to the
sharing of skills or the relinquishment of traditional powers required in this approach.

Within the programmes themselves, we have had
to look closely at our relationships with families
and our expectations for their involvement. Retrospectively, our initial efforts with families were
more instructive and directive than our approach
today. Like other professionals in the community,
we underestimated the contributions that families
made to the development of their children and we
overestimated our contributions. Our approach to
families has changed over the years and these
changes will continue as we learn - both parents and
professionals - how best we can share our skills and
work together more effectively.

Although there have been no simple resolutions
to these problems, positive changes are occurring:
many agencies which were antagonistic are now referring children; more professionals are sharing
skills, if for no other reason than the current
economic climate, which inhibits growth; and research is providing us with a strong rationale and
the tools to enhance parent-professional working
relationships (eg. Bromwich, 1981).

One major advantage these programmes have had,
in comparison with most services which operate in
British Columbia or elsewhere, is that from the
beginning there has been a sense of comradeship and
sharing among staff, parents and societies involved.

The programmes were fortunate that the provincial
government appointed a Provincial Steering Committee
early in the development of this service to ensure
that standards were established and a spirit of co-
operation generated. Early intervention through and
with parents was and is such a new and challenging
field that close, cooperative relationships are
essential in the home, in the community and at the
provincial level.

NOTES

1.   Editors' footnote: Public health nurses
are the equivalent of Health Visitors in Britain.

REFERENCES

Accardo, P.J. and Capute, A.J. (1980) Paediatric
    Education and the Needs of Exceptional
    Children. Baltimore: University Park Press
Bricker, D. (1976) "Educational synthesizer". In
    Hey, Don't Forget About Me. Vancouver: Council
    for Exceptional Children
Bromwich, R.M. (1981) Working with Parents and
    Infants: An Interactional Approach. Baltimore:
    University Park Press
Brynelsen, D.L. (1982) Problems Experienced by Line
    Staff in the Management of Children with
    Multiple Handicaps. Vancouver: University of
    British Columbia Press. (In press)
Kearsley, R.B. (1979) Iatrogenic retardation: a
    syndrome of learned incompetence. In R.B.
    Kearsley and I.E. Sigel (eds.) Infants at Risk:
    Assessment of Cognitive Functioning.
    Hillsdale, N.J.: Lawrence Erlbaum Associates
Sheps, S.B. and Robinson, G.C. (1979) Children with
    Developmental Handicaps: Is There a Gap Between
    Suspicion and Referral? Vancouver: Department
    of Paediatrics, University of British Columbia
Tolleson, L. (1978) Parents' beliefs, attitudes and
    values and their relationship to home environ-
    ment provided for developmentally delayed
    infants involved in a home-based intervention
    programme. Unpublished thesis, University of
    British Columbia

Chapter 5

EARLY SUPPORT AND INTERVENTION: THE HARC INFANT PROGRAMME

Cliff Cunningham

BACKGROUND

The Hester Adrian Research Centre infant research programme began in October 1973. It has focussed on infants with Down's syndrome but has also included 25 infants with other mentally handicapping conditions. Initially we wrote to paediatricians outlining our research and requesting referrals of those parents who were willing to co-operate. At first referrals were rather sparse and confined to particular doctors. However, as parents involved in the research returned to their paediatricians with positive statements, the referral rate increased rapidly. This was aided considerably when we requested referrals from the health visiting service and even more so when a health visitor was seconded to the research team. Over 200 families with a child with Down's syndrome have so far taken part in the programme. The majority have been referred by paediatricians and health visitors and about ten per cent are self-referrals. We publicise as much as possible that we are an open-referral system and that any parents may refer themselves to us. This is important as it assumes that parents have the right to seek help for themselves and their infants and that they do not require the permission of a professional.

From Spring 1974 until August 1980, all infants with Down's syndrome born in Greater Manchester, and whose natural or foster parents wished to be involved in the research, were included. Subsequent enquiries of health visitors, developmental assessment clinics and pre-school and school facilities have indicated that 85 to 90 per cent of infants with the condition born in the area during this time are in the sample. These, together with two dozen

or so families from neighbouring districts, make up
the total sample of infants.

BROAD AIMS AND ORIENTATION

The broad aim of our research is to investigate the
development of infants with Down's syndrome in order
to improve their early stimulation and care. Our
aim is not merely to develop and to assess the effi-
cacy of specific training activities for the infant.
We strongly believe that those engaged in early
intervention must seek to foster opportunities for
the family as a whole to flourish. Thus we are as
concerned with family dynamics, attitudes and
resources as we are with the developmental curriculum; and as concerned with the nature of the service provision as with experimental design. Whilst
we acknowledge that resource limitations make such
aims appear unrealistic, nevertheless we feel that
to concentrate purely on developmental training for
the infant is of limited value and may have harmful
consequences for the family in some circumstances.
     Our conviction is based on the fact that mental
handicap presents a multi-variable set of problems
in relation to cause, consequence and treatments and
that considerable variations are found within the
range of individual children and their families.
Consequently, it is unlikely that a standard treatment can be specified which will be generally
applicable to all the children, parents or families.
Even where a system of treatments is designed, this
must include a great deal of flexibility to meet and
cope with the many changing variables. We also feel
that we lack sufficient knowledge of content and
method in early intervention to define with confidence - except in the broadest sense - specific
treatments and approaches. For example, as will be
discussed later, we would seriously question whether
infant training activities derived from current developmental tests are sufficient, or even valid, as
a base for the curriculum for many mentally handicapped children.

ORGANISATION AND METHODOLOGY

To meet these aims and to cope with this diversity,
we feel that the approach has to be longitudinal,
and responsive to growth and change in the child and
in the family over the years. It has to be concerned with the many variables that impinge on the situation and it must observe this in as natural a sett-

92

ing as possible, i.e. the home and the community.
For us, this comprises four stages:

1. We try initially to observe over a range of
    variables in as natural a setting as possible,
    with the purpose of identifying pertinent
    factors.
2. From these observations we formulate hypotheses
    for testing with an emphasis on experimental
    manipulation. Thus we apply the principle that
    in order to understand change or development,
    one needs to try to influence it, and then to
    evaluate its rate and direction. One important
    aspect of this is parent comment on the inter-
    vention we provide. Equally, we do not dis-
    courage parents seeking other available serv-
    ices, but instead monitor this as an important
    source of information.
3. From such experiments and observations, we
    attempt to formulate models to guide future
    research or practice, and to develop dissem-
    ination procedures. We would argue that re-
    searchers who advocate early intervention pro-
    grammes must be accountable and must demon-
    strate both effectiveness and efficiency, with
    respect to short and long term gains, for par-
    ents, service agencies and, of course, the in-
    fants involved. Therefore:
4. We try to evaluate these action models in the
    field under existing conditions of service
    provision.

    The core of our research is the 'cohort' of
infants with Down's syndrome and their families and
our research activities centre on a home-visiting
programme that includes as a minimum:

1. One or more 'first' visits as soon as possible
    after the diagnosis has been disclosed.
2. Regular six weekly home visits from six weeks
    of age until 78 weeks of age, which incorp-
    orate assessment, support and advice on stimu-
    lation.
3. Home visits at 12 weekly intervals until two
    years. These maintain the support and advice
    but begin to 'wean' parents away from the pro-
    gramme and encourage them to seek out other
    support and advice services such as playgroups,
    opportunity groups or schools.
4. Home visits at six monthly intervals until
    five years of age. These essentially collect

follow-up data of mental development but also
provide, within the context of a one and a half
to three hour visit, some advice and guidance
in response to parent questions.

Throughout these five years all parents are
told repeatedly that we are available for consultation on any issue at any time. They initiate
these consultations by telephone or in writing. In
cases of bereavement we always try to maintain some
contact and carry out at least one home visit
approximately two to three weeks after the child's
death.
    Our complement of staff has grown during the
programme and so the primary visitor, i.e. the one
who carries out the majority of home visits in the
first year or so, has varied since the research
began. The first 46 infants were visited alternatively by myself and another developmental psychologist; the next 55 families were visited by a health
visitor attached to the project. This was a repli-
cation study of our early intervention.
    Since then we have had two postgraduate stud-
ents carrying out investigations requiring one, two
or three weekly visiting. The core staff, however,
carry out all the six weekly visits and we have en-
deavoured to ensure continuity of visits to individual families by the primary visitor. This was
based on the assumption that it would be organis-
ationally simpler and more beneficial to the stimulation programme and to the parent if the same home
visitor carried out the visits. During recent
studies involving several home visitors, however, we
have noted that whereas the primary visitor felt all
was progressing well - as indicated by the general
comments and discussion during the visit - when a
'new' visitor made the visit some parents would reiterate their fears and concerns. In some cases,
this appeared to be no more than the parent 'making
conversation', assuming the visitor would be interested. In others, it was a definite need for parents, and we can only conclude that they assume
repetition of their worries to the familiar primary
visitor will be inappropriate. Also, the new
visitor would often raise some queries over the
stimulation programme, suggesting alternative
approaches or making novel observations. Thus we
are beginning to feel that the best home visitor
service is built around a team who have shared
skills and close communication. Each has a caseload and is the primary visitor, but visits by other

members are systematically built into the programme. This notion is similar to that of the 'named person' or 'key worker' but incorporates recognition of the importance of a team sharing common objectives and techniques but with varying skills and backgrounds.

With the exception of some specific experimental manipulation, all staff in our research who carry out home visits do use similar approaches and share the same philosophy. The importance of a consensus of method and philosophy must be emphasised. Conflicting advice from professionals usually causes parents a great deal of anxiety and can lead to disillusionment with or even rejection of service provisions.

HOME VISITING: PHILOSOPHY AND METHOD

The first tenet of our approach is to endeavour to set up an equal partnership with the parent. This is usually done in the 'first visits' when father is present. We state that as babies are all very individual and because parents have close and continued contact with the baby, it is they who will acquire the expert knowledge about their baby. We, on the other hand, have knowledge about Down's syndrome and development, and we have contact with many babies. This provides us with our expertise and credentials. Thus *together* we will try to ensure that the baby is given every opportunity to develop.

The second tenet is best exemplified by contrasting two polarised 'models': the 'consumer model' and the 'transplant model' (I am grateful to Dorothy Jeffree for this second tag). In the 'consumer model' it is held that:

1. Because each of us brings our own set of knowledge and abilities to new situations, parents are already likely to have some knowledge and skills which are required for the stimulation of their infant.
2. Because each family and parent will react differently to the birth of a handicapped baby - influenced by past experiences, present family circumstances, aspirations, values and attitudes - they will have different needs and requirements.
3. Whilst a large part of our 'sales offer' to parents concerns teaching and therapeutic techniques, parents are not professionals. For example, one can expect a professional to be reasonably objective and objectively

reasonable, ie. one can expect a professional
to make observations and decisions without too
many emotional overtones, and to use factual
knowledge in coming to a relatively realistic
solution. But being a parent means responding
to unreasonable demands (from the professional
viewpoint) from your child: this is one factor
that makes the relationship unique to the
child. Similarly, being the child's parent
gives you the socially legitimate right to make
unreasonable demands for your child.

In the 'consumer model' we do not try to change the
consumer (the parent) into a professional teacher;
we do not attempt to 'transplant' professional
skills into the home so that professional therapies
per se are maintained and extended via the parent.
To do this is to risk 'rejection' of the intervention. Instead we offer parents what we feel is
the necessary information for them to live with and
help their infant with Down's syndrome. They then
select from this according to their current needs
and in their own time.
    We believe that this approach compensates for
our lack of knowledge of the requirements of
families and the efficiency of techniques, and hopefully prevents our imposing too stressful a regime
on the family. In a sense, the approach is experimental rather than prescriptive and dogmatic. It
also implies that the families are responsible for
themselves and their children: the parent is responsible for acquiring the information needed.
    Thus the parent is the consumer and, like any
consumer, can accept or reject our 'goods'. In
such a model, consumer satisfaction becomes an
important variable to monitor, and has strongly
influenced our approach.
    We also hope that this model ensures we remain
firmly in the servicing and advisory role and do not
fall into the trap of 'professional authoritar-
ianism'. This can only lead either to parents rejecting our services or to their becoming too
dependent upon our services (Sandow and Clarke,
1978). Some years ago my attention was drawn to
that eminent developmental text 'House at Pooh
Corner' and the following passage:

    It was going to be one of Rabbit's busy days.
    As soon as he woke up he felt important, as
    if everything depended upon him. It was just
    the day for Organising Something, or for

96

Writing a Notice Signed Rabbit, or for Seeing
What Everybody Else Thought About It.   It was
a perfect morning for hurrying round to see
Pooh, and saying "Very well, then, I'll tell
Piglet", and then going to Piglet and saying,
"Pooh thinks - but perhaps I'd better see Owl
first".   It was a Captainish sort of day, when
everybody said, "Yes, Rabbit", and "No,
Rabbit", and waited until he had told them.

(From A.A. Milne, House at Pooh Corner,
Methuen, 1926)

Human experts and rabbits have much in common.
Firstly, they multiply at a prolific rate. Secondly, they are both highly susceptible to infection;
rabbits catch myxamatosis and experts catch expertosis. The symptoms are common to both: the head
swells and the patient goes blind. So as we visit
more families in the course of intervention programmes, we increase our confidence and expertise
and with this the risk of expertosis. Suddenly we
begin to pre-empt and short-cut parent questions.
We stop manifestly working through developmental
problems with parents, explaining our observations
and analyses as we go; instead, we recognise some
increasingly familiar cue and are likely to produce
an increasingly familiar recipe for action. But
this is in opposition to one of our basic aims. If
parents are to be independent, they need to be able
to do their own programming. Thus they need to
'consume' or 'internalise' the teaching approach
that we apply in developing training activities
(Cunningham and Jeffree, 1971). To do this it is
essential that the parent is constantly encouraged
to understand why the activity is important for the
child, to invent and augment the ideas of how it can
best be carried out and to observe for themselves
the progress being made from which to make their own
decisions for change. It is too easy and too comfortable to provide packaged recipes for action
which do not require parent involvement at this
level.
   We do not know which parental characteristics
are most essential to this increasing independence.
My impression is that parents generally can quickly
acquire and improve the major elements of the experimental teaching approach: objective observation,
task analysis, presentation procedures (both direct
as in behaviour modification or indirect as in play
therapy) and evaluation and reappraisal. We believe

that home visitors should consciously decrease their
input of these skills and encourage parents to take
over. What is more difficult is the content of the
stimulation. Parents generally do not have the
depth of developmental knowledge required to select
appropriate teaching goals. Reliance on simple
checklists may be a current practical necessity but
it is by no means sufficient; a far greater knowledge of early developmental processes is needed.
    What then do we do? We cannot give the parent
a crash course in development and education which
will suffice all needs throughout early childhood,
let alone later life, even if the knowledge were
readily available. Parents are going to require
continuing advice on the content of treatment and
management as the child grows and changes. Thus we
aim to prepare parents to seek out this advice by
increasing their confidence and skill in dealing
with professionals. This comes about through positive experiences gained with the home visiting team,
with increased use of a professional vocabulary and
concepts, and is aided by explanations of professional roles and expectations, and in some cases, our
direct intervention as mediators between parents an
other professions. Recently several professionals
and students who have had short attachments to the
programme have expressed surprise at the parents'
questions and dealings with them; as one social
worker put it, "They have obviously been well trained at coping with us". Schools are also beginning
to feel the challenge of such knowledgeable parents,
especially when closely questioned about objectives
and individual teaching programmes.
    We aim, then, to augment parenting skills and
not merely 'transplant' our own teaching and therapeutic values and techniques into the home. During
the course of this, we attempt to minimise stress
on the parent and family. Parents are often anxious that they are not doing enough or that they
are directly contributing to the handicap through
poor management. This is virtually inevitable,
given the underlying concept of behavioural and
stimulation programmes that control over environmental factors can have a great effect on the
child's level of functioning. We attempt to set up
a partnership with the parents based on mutual
respect for each others' expertise and skills and
try to avoid making assumptions and value judgements on what parents should and should not do.
Instead, we try to maintain the role of a consumer
service; the infant is their infant not ours. We

appreciate that parents should be as independent of the services as possible in their teaching and management, but equally we realise that they will need the services to provide practical resources and support and knowledge on many occasions throughout the child's life.

Thus we aim to provide:

. information and training on how parents can devise and carry out activities to aid the child's development;
. advice on the management of health difficulties which are likely to be associated with Down's syndrome, such as feeding, diet and respiratory problems;
. advice on management of behavioural difficulties when necessary;
. accurate information about Down's syndrome which includes the causes, risk rates, mortality and short and long term prospects;
. information about local and national support services, both voluntary and statutory;
. advice on how to use the services, including preparing parents in advance with realistic expectations of service provisions;
. liaison between the parent and other services;
. last, but not least, we provide emotional support.

In relation to these goals, our intervention programme can be seen as having three phases. The first centres on the 'first visits' and the parents learning to "accept and come to terms with" the handicap. This is followed by a phase which aims at helping the parent to acquire and to develop the knowledge and skills needed to organise and carry out stimulation activities. The third phase, the 'weaning' phase, is near the end of the 18 months to two years and aims to help parents move on to other services.

These natural phases in the programme reflect the changing needs of the family following the birth of an infant with Down's syndrome. In the first year we have found three distinct phases which are common to the majority of families - particularly the mothers (Cunningham and Sloper, 1977). The first we tag the 'traumatic period' and this usually lasts from a few days following the disclosure to about 12 weeks. Our intervention at this time accepts that many parents are likely to have a *grief reaction* or *psychic crisis* to the disclosure (see Figure 1).

We visit the family as often as required during this phase and spend the majority of our time explaining causes, consequences, treatment, and future possibilities. We always try to provide the parent with some practical activities and advice - usually on handling and strength exercises - as our experience suggests that this will help to speed up their passage through this period. As with grief reactions to bereavement, one should not try to deny, ignore or reduce this reaction, as it does appear important for many parents. During the early visits one needs to allow parents to reiterate fears and the intervener needs to be ready patiently to repeat points previously covered. My concern here is that whilst we appear to do this with most mothers during our regular visits, we usually only see those fathers whose work allows them to be at home and who are willing to meet us. I cannot discuss fathers to any great extent here but two points need to be considered. Firstly, my experience suggests that fathers are more likely to have difficulties in accepting the condition and secondly, many fathers seem to prefer discussing the problems of adjustment with a man during this first phase. I would also note that whilst we see both parents together at the first visit, it is often useful to see parents separately by discretely managing one's visiting, particularly if parents are still debating whether to take the baby home or not.

An essential point in this first period, which occurs in the adaptation or the orientation phase, is when the new infant begins to establish a behavioural interaction with the parent. We have carried out a number of studies in this area (Berger, 1981) and as a result we prepare the parents for the slower emergence of eye-gaze and smiling at about nine to 12 weeks. We also try to teach the parents how to improve the phasing of their behaviour to that of the infant: in most cases this requires parents to pause longer between emitting a signal and expecting the infant's reaction. This process can also be aided by telling parents just to imitate the infant's behaviours, thus ensuring that the parents give the infant time to respond, or to send out a behaviour to which parents then immediately respond. As yet we are unable to provide objective evidence that these interventions are necessary or useful, but anecdotally there are many supportive cases. For example, whilst counselling the parents of an 18 week old infant with Down's syndrome who

Figure 5.1: Model of Psychic Crisis at Disclosure of Handicap

PARENT IS TOLD	PSYCHIC CRISIS	Manifestations		Needs
	SHOCK PHASE	Emotional disorganisation confusion, paralysis of actions, disbelief, irrationality	) Can last) from 2) minutes to) several) days.	Sympathy and emotional support
Frequent oscillation between phases	REACTION PHASE	Expression of: sorrow, grief, disappointment, anxiety, aggression, denial, guilt, failure, defence mechanisms	) A process) of rein-) tegration) through) discussion.	Listen to parent. Catharsis through talking out. Sympathy but honesty. Facts on cause
	ADAPTATION PHASE	Realistic appraisal: parents ask 'What can be done?' This is a *signal of readiness* to proceed with 'How can we help?'		Reliable and accurate information on medical and educational treatment and future
	ORIENTATION PHASE	Parents begin to organise, seek help and information, plan for future		Provision of regular help and guidance in treatment
	CRISIS OVER			Appropriate provision of services

From: Cunningham, C.C. (1979) Parent counselling. In: Tredgold's Mental Retardation, 12th Edition.
Edited by Craft, M. London: Ballière Tindall

had not received any support or advice, I explained the slower maturation of the nervous system, the slower processing abilities and the slower rates of transmission along the nerves. This, I argued, meant that we should alter our natural interactive phasing and slow it down. I then gave the infant to mother and asked her to imitate the baby, to wait longer for responses and generally "switch to second gear" (I had mentioned she seemed to be in overdrive most of the time, probably because she was so anxious to help the baby). Within a minute or so, she had begun to elicit consistent smiling and vocalisations from the infant. She hugged the baby to her breast and beamed at her husband. (I assume this is what is meant by bonding.)

Our observations indicate that this first stage is coming to an end when the parent begins to get more satisfying interactions with the baby, due largely to the developmental changes in the infant, and it is often signalled by parents referring to the baby by name rather than by 'the baby' (Cunningham and Sloper, 1977).

However, in most cases there is a functional acceptance of the condition at this time; the parent is ready to face most days and challenges and is ready to learn how to help the infant. I do not know whether parents ever totally accept the condition - or whether they should (Cunningham, 1982).

The next period (three to 10 months) we tag the 'euphoric phase'. Parents (mothers) often begin to tell us that "the baby is as quick as my others" or that "he's just as quick as next door's baby". They say that he or she is really like any baby, not what they expected. "Perhaps she will be a 'bright one'." This is the period when the parents appear to be most open to learning the new observational and analytical skills of the intervention.

A typical visit during this period begins with an assessment of the infant's developmental level. We use the Bayley Scales of Infant Development (Bayley, 1969) as this provides us with standardised data for research purposes. From an intervention viewpoint, a reasonably detailed checklist is sufficient. It will pin-point the infants' current level of development and those behaviours which might reasonably be expected to develop next. We insist that parents observe these assessments. I cannot stress sufficiently that these 'checklist' assessments act purely to focus attention on the developmental areas and create a set of initial situations within which to interact with the child.

They do not constitute the sole means of identifying behavioural goals. From these assessments, we set up a number of possible training methods in discussion with the parent, taking care to explain the developmental significance of the selected behaviours across different aspects of development.

For example, the baby who can sit up not only can use his or her hands to play and to explore and has a wider range of visual opportunities, but is more likely to engage in social interactions. Similarly, we explain that putting cubes in cups or boxes serves to extend the infant's span of attention as well as to open up new games and motor activities to facilitate these behaviours and explore how these work with the infant. This usually acts as a demonstration and during it we note the effect of using prompts, rewards, cueing and phasing. On many occasions we then ask the parent to try it out and can correct the parent's behaviour. (It must be noted that these are guidelines and not every guideline is automatically applied to every behaviour or every parent every time.)

In our first group of 46 infants we did not provide written instructions for these activities, but parents were encouraged to take notes. Occasionally they would request a written explanation for fathers, and as memory aids for themselves. The parents who did this however were less than five per cent of the sample. In the next group of parents, the health visitor wrote down detailed explanations of the behavioural goals and how to carry them out for all visits. However when next visited, many of the parents could not find the notes easily and most admitted that they seldom referred to them.

Recent groups have been given more detailed, typed booklets of activities and these are referred to during visits; parents are also given recording sheets to note when and how often they carried out an activity. We are currently assessing the effect of this more structured and organised approach but our impression is that no significant effects are reflected in the developmental scores of the different groups at 18 months to two years. Certainly no significant developmental differences were found between the mental ages of the first and second groups.

We try to inform parents of management and training techniques as part of the immediate stimulation activities and we explain the significance of developmental processes of the selected behaviours. We also discuss attitudes and philosophies of child rearing. We do not impose a strict training regime of so many minutes a day, or a set number of training sessions on the parent (except in some recent experimental manipulations). Instead, we try to emphasise that they can do much of the necessary stimulation during their every-day interactions with the infant. In other words we avoid centering all the mother's or family's activities on the stimulation programme and instead try to emphasise the use of the ideas or skills within the daily regime. Hopefully, this maintains the balance within the family and avoids, to some extent, a sudden concentration of effort on the infant at the expense of other family members and activities.

Following the 'assessment and training' part of the visit we relax with the parent, usually over a cup of tea, and talk about various matters. We see this as an essential part of the intervention but we do not formalise it to the parent. The purpose of our visit is the 'assessment and training', not counselling for stress or problems. This comes about in a more indirect manner. Wherever possible, we avoid direct questions about likely difficulties unless the problem has been voiced and discussed previously. I clearly remember the consensus of outrage of a group of parents when one noted that the opening remark of a social worker was, "Well, what problems have you got?". Why, they asked, do so many people think you have to have problems just because the child has a handicapping condition. We always try to answer all questions honestly. If information is not known we frankly admit it but also say that we will try to find out.

We are also very sensitive about ending our visits. We try not to stay too long as there are enough disruptions to family routines at this time. Usually visits last from one and a half to three hours. Care is also taken not to appear to hurry away from the visit as our experience has indicated that the issue which is really worrying the parent is often raised as one is about to leave.

This visit pattern is fairly typical throughout the two years, but varies with the changes in the parent. As noted earlier, we aim to withdraw more and more from talking about 'how to teach' the baby as parents increase their skills. However, in the early visits we try very hard not to make the parents feel incompetent at coping with their baby. A major worry of all new parents of a handicapped child is, "Will we cope?". The home intervener must give the parent confidence to cope, not prove how good the intervener is with the infant at the expense of the parent. Thus there are no obvious cut-offs or changes in our parent training, just a series of subtle adaptations. By seven to 12 months, most parents will quite suddenly 'see' the handicap. Their baby will be next to another; and they will compare and 'see' the delay. This is usually a gross motor activity, like sitting. At this stage, one needs again to be ready to discuss worries about the future. It is not as manifestly traumatic as the initial phase and is often over-looked.

I must also note that around this fourth quarter of the first year, the babies often begin to develop more independence and are less willing to be taught. It is no longer easy to physically prompt a hand movement, as they begin to resist. If they wish to get on their feet and bounce about, it is difficult, and possibly not appropriate, to make them sit and post shapes. We try to meet this by again explaining the importance of emotional development, self-initiated activities, exploration and independence, and to begin to help parents organise play situations which will aid development. Indeed, we strongly encourage the parent shifting to more indirect teaching approaches at this stage. This appears to meet the developmental demands of the infant and to reduce stress on the parent.

The beginnings of the toddler stage (18 months to two years) brings further increased independence as well as a new factor - mobility. We now find ourselves advising parents on behavioural management techniques. This stage often leads into the discussion of facilities such as playgroups, nurseries and so on.

CONTENT OF THE DEVELOPMENTAL ACTIVITIES

The details of our curriculum have been published elsewhere (Cunningham and Sloper, 1978). The main feature of our approach is that we take the view that the child's development is the result of interactions between maturational processes and the environment and that this can be influenced by specific deficiencies. These deficiencies can arise in the sensory systems, e.g. vision, hearing, etc.; or at the cognitive level in impaired learning and information processing. Thus the role of the intervener is to try to weigh up these influences for each set of developmental activities and to seek appropriate treatments.

We view development, particularly in the child with Down's syndrome, as taking the form of a series of spurts and plateaux in which there are times when the child is more likely to be sensitive to and react to intervention than others. These times normally coincide with a spurt forward in development. The plateaux coincide with either maturational waiting periods or consolidation periods of newly acquired skills; that is, the infant rehearses and adapts a skill across a range of environmental situations. We view development as having both vertical and horizontal components and hence, intervention need not, and possibly should not, be a continuous process.

This is important for parents. For example, in our first group of families we often found parents becoming very disillusioned and self-blaming when little progress was seen to occur in the child. Lack of progress was seen even after we had broken down the tasks into minute steps, tried different teaching strategies and so on. We began to analyse our developmental profiles of the children and found that there were some regularly occurring 'plateaux'. One, for example, is around six to seven months when the child moves from simple play - sucking, banging, pushing and throwing all objects - to relational play where the child begins to use objects together or in a functional manner, e.g. taking out and putting into cups. We surmised that this was a consolidation period when the child needed to spend time rehearsing simple play skills, or alternatively that cognitive development had not progressed sufficiently to allow the next move forward. At this time mothers are advised on tasks which extend the skills sideways (i.e. horizontal) rather than seek to establish the next step up the developmental ladder. During these periods, we encourage mothers to carry out 'probes' on new behaviour so that at the first glimmer that a spurt might be about to take place, she can begin to organise the activities to encourage the development.

Our experience is that parents are very relieved to understand that it is not their poor teaching or lack of effort that is causing the apparent halt in development, but the child's own maturational programme.

Similarly, we emphasise that mentally handicapped babies are born with great innate variations in ability and personality. Thus not all parents can have the brightest Down's syndrome baby. I find that parents, though disappointed, are comforted by this. Unfortunately, many early intervention programmes have published results in high euphoria which, when diluted through various dissemination and media channels, have proclaimed that great bene-fits for potentially severely mentally handicapped infants will result from early structured stimu-lation. Kysela (1974), as only one example, empha-sised the comparability of motor co-ordination and communication skills of Down's syndrome children to the attainments expected of any child of the same chronological age, when reporting on his visit to the Washington Down's Syndrome Programme. Clunies-Ross (1979) refers to the same programme and reports that at five years of age the children are achieving 95 per cent of tasks expected of normal children of the same age. Whilst this is true for a small min-ority, our results strongly indicate a tremendous range of ability regardless of the early inter-vention provided. We have children with measured intelligence in the normal range (i.e. mental ages of four to five) at five years, and others who have been given as much care and help who have mental ages of 12 to 18 months. Thus we must not lose sight of the nature of the handicap in our desire to help. There are limits to what can be achieved and whilst we must continually test these limits we must, at the same time, maintain a realistic picture for parents.

CONCLUSION

I have tried to emphasise that great individual differences are found in mentally handicapped child-ren, even those with a similar condition like Down's syndrome. Great individual differences are also found in mothers, in fathers, in families; in homes and in communities; in individuals' resources, abilities, attitudes and interests. Thus, whatever we do, our approach has to be flexible, tolerant and open to change. Providing we do this, there can be little doubt that early intervention is of great importance to the family and to the mentally handicapped infant.

REFERENCES

Bayley, N. (1969) Bayley Scales of Infant Develop-ment. New York: The Psychological Corporation
Berger, J. (1981) Early development of social sig-nalling, attentional and communicative behav-iours in Down's syndrome and non-handicapped

infants. Unpublished Ph.D. thesis, University of Manchester

Clunies-Ross, C.G. (1979) Accelerating the development of Down's syndrome infants and young children. Journal of Special Education, 13, 169-177

Cunningham, C.C. (1979) Early stimulation of the mentally handicapped child. In M. Craft (ed.) Tredgold's Mental Retardation, 12th Edition. London: Ballière Tindall

Cunningham, C.C. (1982) Down's Syndrome: An Introduction for Parents. London: Souvenir Press

Cunningham, C.C. and Jeffree, D.M. (1971) Working with Parents: Developing a Workshop Course for Parents of Young Mentally Handicapped Children. Manchester: The National Society for Mentally Handicapped Children (North West Region)

Cunningham, C.C. and Sloper, P. (1977) Down's syndrome: a positive approach to parent and professional collaboration. Health Visitor, 50, 32-37

Cunningham, C.C. and Sloper, P. (1978) Helping Your Handicapped Baby. London: Souvenir Press

Kysela, G.M. (1974) Early childhood education for children with Down's syndrome. Mental Retardation Bulletin, 2, 58-63

Sandow, S. and Clarke, A.D.B. (1978) Home intervention with parents of severely subnormal, pre-school children: an interim report. Child: Care, Health and Development, 4, 29-39

DISCUSSION

Because of their similar subjects, papers four and five were discussed together. Dana Brynelsen gave some extra examples of the practical implementation of the philosophy behind the British Columbia Infant Development Programmes. Group meetings include mothers' and toddlers' groups once or twice weekly, evening classes (e.g. on language development) and parents' meetings for mutual support. She also described the involvement of "pilot-parents", who themselves have a handicapped child, and who undertake to visit the parents of a newly-diagnosed handicapped child who say they would welcome such contact. Several participants expressed enthusiasm for such a service, suggesting that, for example, it can help fathers to adjust more quickly, and counteract a family's feelings of isolation. However, a number of caveats were mentioned. It must not be forgotten that the parents usually first have thought the child was normal, and that it takes time to accept the new identity of 'parent of a handicapped child'. The parents may feel under pressure to accept the services offered, and may rather need to be protected from too many visitors at this early stage. There may be a problem, particularly when the diagnosis is uncertain, of parents seeing the pilot-parent's child as the model for their own child's future development.

Cliff Cunningham commented that about half of the parents in the HARC Infant Project did not want (or retrospectively would not have wanted) to meet other parents at an early stage. Philippa Russell made the point that families have changing needs, as well as differing needs, and that at some times they may want special services, and at other times to concentrate on ordinary things. It was also noted that 'adjusting to the child's handicap' should not ideally be such an enormous and traumatic step. Society has the responsibility of accepting and not devaluing handicapped people.

Cliff Cunningham commented further on some of the ways in which relationships between parents and professionals may become estranged. He suggested that, as well as our recognizing the responsibilities of professionals, parents too have some responsibility and must be expected to be sympathetic in their dealings with professionals. In turn, professionals must make clear that they are not in a hurry when visiting parents, and ensure that parents know they can always get in touch. The HARC Infant Project staff give parents their home phone numbers, and find that it certainly does build up parents' confidence yet leads only to infrequent calls.

Discussion then centred on fostering and respite care. Dana Brynelsen noted that five to ten per cent of participants in the B.C. Infant Development Programmes are not the natural parents of the child, i.e. foster parents in most cases. Cliff Cunningham estimated that in ten to fifteen per cent of cases known to his research, the natural parents had not taken the Down's syndrome baby home with them from hospital. Many do eventually take the baby home; the project had a number of such cases which clearly showed that counselling about the causes and future development, and the promise of a regular home visiting service which would provide guidance and support were influential in helping the parents decide. The time parents took to make the decision was also reduced. In several cases, after

a three-to-four hour counselling session when
questions were answered, the parents went to collect
the baby within 24 hours. However, not all parents
do this - with or without counselling - and about
ten per cent of the sample are fostered. The foster
parents are then involved in the early intervention
programmes.

Despite active participation in an intervention
programme and good relationships with professionals,
some families find the child brings many pressures
on them. But they may recoil from the notion of
sharing the care with others. In the HARC Infant
Project, the staff have begun to encourage parents
to consider the use of shared care as a *positive*
resource. It is emphasised that the notion of
independence and being as 'normal' as possible will
mean that the child will eventually leave home and
live in the community or a sheltered environment.
Thus they need, like any child, to get used to
this. Staying overnight with a friend or relative,
school trips etc. are all part of this process. In
some cases where parents find it particularly difficult, they may be too tired to realise that they
are getting close to a crisis. Hence the regular
use of shared care, either with relatives or short
term fostering (e.g. occasional weekends with
another family) will give parents a chance to consider how things are. In this sense, respite or
shared care becomes a positive aspect of intervention for both parents and children, and not a
desperate result of what the parent sees as his or
her own failure.

Chapter 6

DEVELOPING PARTNERSHIP: THE ANSON HOUSE PRESCHOOL PROJECT

Sally Beveridge

INTRODUCTION

The Anson House Preschool Project is one of a number
of projects at the Hester Adrian Research Centre,
University of Manchester. It began in 1975 as a
service and research project concerned with pre-
school mentally handicapped children and their
families. It is funded primarily by Dr. Barnardo's,
with additional support from Manchester Education
Committee, and since 1981, from Manchester Area
Health Authority. Initially the project team consisted of psychologists and teachers: over time the
need for multidisciplinary service provision became
apparent, and the current team comprises two
teachers, a nursery nurse, three psychologists and a
social worker. In addition, regular input is made
to the project by a speech therapist and physiotherapist, and close links have been established
with a range of specialist services within the community.
  Since 1977 a special feature of the project has
been the integration of children of widely differing
developmental abilities within the classroom group.
The development of classroom provision for groups of
preschool children ranging from those who are profoundly retarded and multiply handicapped, through
those with less severe handicap, to children who
show no developmental delay has been described by
Gunstone, Hogg, Sebba, Warner and Almond (1982).
Children who attend the project are drawn from the
City of Manchester, and are referred by a range of
professionals including preschool teachers, paediatricians, health visitors and social workers, or
families may refer themselves. Currently twelve
children, eight of whom are handicapped and four
non-handicapped, attend Anson House on four mornings

a week. One parent of each child (usually the mother) is asked to attend one session per week so that we can work together with the children. In practice most parents attend more frequently, many attending almost as often as their children.

The model of parent involvement in Anson House has gradually been developed through the experience of working together practically with the parents and their children who have participated in the project. This paper will summarize the changes which have taken place in our approach to parental involvement over time, the current model and the day-to-day service provision. Finally new directions in the work to be undertaken at Anson House are raised.

THE STARTING POINT (1975-1977)

When the Anson House Preschool Project started in 1975 there was already wide recognition that in order for early intervention schemes to be really effective, professionals needed to involve the parents as fully as possible. Bronfenbrenner (1976), in his influential review of Head Start programmes, noted that it was only when parents had been actively involved that there was evidence of lasting intervention effects. With the benefit of hindsight, his findings concur with common sense: for most young children the parents remain the primary caretakers and the home is their primary environment. No matter how intensive professional intervention may be, it is clear that the family home environment is of vital importance to the child's development. Moreover, it has been demonstrated that parents could be effective teachers of their own children (e.g. O'Dell, 1974; Cunningham, 1975).

The project at Anson House therefore started with the explicit aim of providing educational intervention for preschool mentally handicapped children both directly, through programmed work in a classroom context, and indirectly, through parent-teaching work. We knew that we could not hope to achieve very much, particularly given our limited contact time with the children, unless we developed a consistent approach between home and Anson House: in other words, we as professionals needed parental cooperation in order to put our own intervention schemes into most effective practice.

From the outset then, parents were asked to participate in the project by attending at least one session per week, so that discussion of their children and the educational programmes that had been devised, as well as joint observation and assessment of their children could take place. The first formal parent-teaching courses began in 1977.

THE CHANGING FRAMEWORK (1977-1980)

Through the experience of working practically together with the parents and their children, we became aware of the necessity of meeting a wide range of parents' needs. This led to changes both in our theoretical approach to intervention, and in the practicalities of the project's day-to-day service provision. At a theoretical level, we moved increasingly towards an ecological approach to intervention (Hogg, 1979). This position makes explicit the importance of taking full account of all the social settings in which an individual participates. Most obvious of these for the children at Anson House is the home, but other settings include playgroups, schools and hospitals. In practical terms, the appointment of a social worker to join the project team enabled closer and more effective links to be established, not only between Anson House and home but also with community services.

Thus, from an initial focus on the child as client, we were moving towards service provision for the families of the children, including social work intervention and community liaison as well as parent-teaching work. At the same time, integration of the children's classroom provision began to be matched by integration of the service to families; accordingly, the same service was offered to the families of both handicapped and non-handicapped children who attended the project.

By this stage, parents were seen by the project staff not just as recipients of professional help and advice but also as full partners in the intervention process. This partnership emphasised the need to bring together parents' in-depth knowledge and intimate relationship with their own children with the project staff's broader perspective e.g. of child development and educational methods, in order to best facilitate the children's development.

PARENTS AS PART OF THE MULTIDISCIPLINARY TEAM (1980+)

As the project's multidisciplinary approach to intervention became established, it was increasingly felt that the parents should be fully and explicitly involved as members of the multidisciplinary team. This resulted in an attempt to define and clarify with the parents not only their role as they saw it but also the roles of the other members of the team in sharing responsibility for the children's development.

If we place too much emphasis on the parents' expertise with their own children without relating it to the complementary expertise of others involved in early childhood development, we run the risk of placing an extreme burden on parents' shoulders by making them feel solely responsible for their child's progress. Thus we have a strong responsibility in our work with parents not only to work together to foster their confidence in their expertise and role as parents, but also to make clear exactly what the roles of the many different 'helping' professions are.

DAY-TO-DAY PARENTAL INVOLVEMENT IN ANSON HOUSE

When their children join the classroom group, parents have already gone through a process of gradual introduction to the project. They will have visited Anson House and seen the classroom in action, and met parents and staff. They will also have been visited by certain of the project staff at home. The social worker makes initial contact with a family and continues home visits until the child joins the project; in her visits she gives information about the project, carries out a social work assessment, and coordinates transport arrangements. A project teacher and psychologist also visit the family in order to discuss the child's development with the parents, and to explore what their priorities for educational intervention for their child are. A play-based assessment of the child also takes place during this visit.

The first months of participation in the project constitute a settling-in phase for both children and parents. Because of the general availability of staff and parents in Anson House, there is opportunity for a great deal of informal discussion as well as for formal meetings which are arranged in order to introduce parents to staff roles and routines within the project.

From this point, and throughout a family's participation in the project, daily contact takes place between parents and classroom staff on all those occasions when a parent attends Anson House; fortnightly meetings are timetabled with speech and physiotherapist where appropriate. The social worker is available in the building for both individual and group discussion, as well as maintaining home visits with each family. Each child is also assigned as the administrative responsibility of one of the psychologists. Administrative responsibility incorporates:

1. Anson House administration: responsibility for explaining and discussing assessments of their child with the parents; responsibility for co-ordinating the decision-making procedure e.g. in termly case conferences; development and monitoring of individual educational programmes both in Anson House and at home.

2. Outside administration: responsibility for liaison with other educational agencies and hospitals with whom families have contact; responsibility for liaison concerning such contacts with the project social worker.

The regular meetings which are timetabled between parents and the psychologist with administrative responsibility include parent-teaching sessions.

Two of the major aims of our service for parents are to increase parents' confidence in their own expertise and knowledge of their children and to increase their information about what it is that different professionals have to offer, and about how the service provision within the community is organised. We are concerned that there should be a smooth transition to community provision for all families when they leave Anson House. Thus, parental involvement in the project begins with intensive support and help where needed, which is gradually faded in intensity as parents feel more confident. By the time a child and family leave the project, they will already have been linked with certain key workers, such as staff of their local school and social services department. For example, they will have visited and have had introductory meetings with teachers in the school to which their child is moving, and the staff of the school will have visited Anson House. Joint observation of the child, and discussion of assessment and programme records takes place at Anson House with parents and local authority staff, who are then invited to participate in the final project case conference.

A continuing transitional service is offered to the parents over the following term after they have left Anson House. This includes liaison with the schools and social services department by project teachers and social worker, and monthly visits at home by the psychologist with administrative responsibility for the family in order to follow through on parent-teaching work.

THE CURRENT SERVICE MODEL

The current service model incorporates social work intervention, liaison with community networks and resources, and parental involvement in educational intervention. This model is influenced by the recognition of certain parental and staff needs.

Parental Needs
Parents of mentally handicapped children have been described as a group under pressure, who share certain needs, anxieties and difficulties. The picture of common needs which emerges from research studies includes:

. the need to understand the nature of their child's handicap more fully;
. the need to know what to expect in the future, not only in terms of their child's development but also in relation to community provision;
. the need for information about aids and appliances which are available, and the allowances and services to which they are entitled;
. the need for introduction to the relevant representatives of voluntary and statutory agencies within the community;
. the need to know what they can do to best facilitate their child's development.

In developing the framework for our service provision, we have been concerned to respond to these expressed needs of parents of mentally handicapped children as a group, while yet remaining aware of the differences in needs between individual parents – differences which relate not only to their preschool handicapped child, but also to a wider family and social environment in which they live. At the same time, and of particular importance to us, has been the aim of developing a model of equal relevance for all the parents involved in Anson House, whether or not their children are handicapped. While recognising the special needs of families with handicapped children, we have attempted to develop an appreciation of the common needs shared by all families of preschool children.

Staff Needs
Anson House staff have identified needs for collaboration with parents in the following areas.

1. <u>Assessment of the children</u>. If we did not have
access to the parents' wealth of information about
their own children, any attempt to draw up an
accurate picture of each child's strengths and weaknesses in different areas of development would be
difficult and time-consuming. Moreover, a comprehensive assessment requires us to take account of
the experiences of those who know the child best and
who know how the child typically behaves in a range
of different contexts.

2. <u>Educational planning and intervention</u>. For
most of the children, their family home is their
primary environment, and one therefore in which
learning must take place. We cannot assume that
skills learned in one context are automatically
generalised to others, either home to Anson House
or Anson House to home. We therefore need to try to
ensure that, together with the parents, we develop a
consistency of approach and a common set of priorities and goals.

3. <u>Social work intervention</u>. In order to involve
parents effectively in the project, we must take
account of the pressures and stresses within individual families. We need to know how the home-
school liaison, mediated by social work involvement,
can help towards a better understanding of the
family's needs by Anson House staff.

The Model for Parental Involvement
The current model incorporates five major areas:
social work support; exchange of information; parent participation; developing parent-child relations; liaison between the children and their
families and community resources.

1. <u>Social work support</u>. For many parents Anson
House is their first encounter with a social worker.
Some parents have not heard of social workers, and
others are often left wondering about the aim and
purpose of their visits. The Anson House social
worker discusses with the families attending the
project whether or not they need any of the following
services to assist them with the care of their child

at home:

1. Provision of information about the availability of national and local services for
   mentally handicapped and preschool children and their families.
2. Advice about the use of services e.g.
   criteria for eligibility, organisational
   functioning in terms of identifying who
   needs to be contacted to ensure effective
   service delivery.
3. Liaison on their behalf with statutory
   and voluntary agencies.
4. Opportunities to clarify and resolve areas
   of difficulty and stress created by the
   child within the family.

2. <u>Exchange of information</u>. Three broad areas can
be described:

1. Information about the project - its philosophy, organisation, and goals.
2. Information about child development, the
   relationship between delayed and non-
   delayed patterns of development, and
   principles of early education.
3. Information about local authority and
   voluntary organisation provision within
   the community.

3. <u>Parent participation within the team</u>. Three
possible levels of involvement in their child's
education may be described:

1. In assessment: parents are always involved in any assessments carried out in
   the project. The purpose of the assessment is discussed beforehand, and the
   meaning of the results afterwards. Parents have continuing access to the individual file in which their child's
   assessment and programme records are
   kept. They are also consulted before
   any such information is passed on to
   outside agencies.
2. In the decision-making process: case conferences are held each term, involving
   both parents, in which the establishment
   of priorities for educational intervention, and the planning of individual
   programme work, are discussed and re-

viewed, and decisions made.

3. In the observation and teaching of their child: one parent from each family is asked to participate in a formal parent-teaching course. Parents meet individually with one of the project psychologists on a weekly basis. Together they select a task which the parent works on at home with his or her child. Each week the parent and child demonstrate how the teaching task is progressing, and the psychologist discusses the use of a range of teaching techniques with the parent.

4. <u>Developing parent-child relationships</u>. In the past years of the project, new parents frequently expressed a lack of confidence that they were "doing the right things" with their young mentally handicapped child. Through the parent-teaching work, parents are made aware of the strategies they are already using in interaction with their child, and are also introduced to other teaching techniques and strategies and to individualised programmes for their own child. The emphasis is on developing consistency and confidence in their own approach.

Through social work intervention, confidence in the parents' abilities or competence and reassurance concerning parent-child relationships are discussed individually within the home setting and informal group discussion at Anson House.

5. <u>Liaison between families and community networks and resources</u>. Because of the complexity surrounding the provision of services, part of the social work task is to act as locator of resources within the community and as interpreter of parents' needs to other community networks and resources. The roles of mediator with unresponsive or poorly functioning networks and of advocate ensuring families receive services for which they are eligible play an important part in the project.

The model outlined here is used as a framework of service provision for all the parents attending Anson House, whether or not their child is handicapped. The different components of the service have been fully described in Beveridge, Flanagan, McConachie and Sebba (1982).

WHERE NEXT?

A major area of concern underlying the development of parental involvement in Anson House relates to how one may best tailor the service provided to fit the needs of individual parents and of the wider family.

Taking parent-teaching work as an example, a study was undertaken during the first phase of the project to explore differences in parents' natural styles of interacting with and teaching their own children. Some parents are naturally more directive than others in their approach, and prefer to intervene actively and to prompt their child's activities. Others are less directive and prefer to set up activities and then sit back to see what their child will do. We have attempted to respect the parents' preferred style of interaction, and take account of these and other differences between parents in developing an individualised approach to parent-teaching work. However, we are aware of a large number of differences between families that have not been taken into account in this work so far.

Where social work intervention and liaison with community networks at Anson House is based on assessment of family needs, the parent-teaching work undertaken so far has been restricted to one parent, usually the mother. The importance of taking account of the structures and routines of family life, and the involvement of other family members than the mother in caring for the child are elaborated by McConachie (Chapter 7, this volume). Future studies in Anson House will seek to explore the following questions: Do parents see teaching as part of their role as parents? Do other family members than the mothers spend time playing with and teaching the children? Does our emphasis on parent-teaching sessions with the child disrupt the established family routine? How can we fit our intervention to meet the needs of an individual family?

REFERENCES

Beveridge, S., Flanagan, R., McConachie, H. and
    Sebba, J. (1982) Parental Involvement in Anson
    House. Anson House Preschool Project Paper 3.
    Barkingside: Barnardo's
Bronfenbrenner, U. (1976) Is early intervention
    effective?: facts and principles of early
    intervention - a summary. In A.M. Clarke and

A.D.B. Clarke (eds.) <u>Early Experience</u>: <u>Myth and Evidence</u>. London: Open Books

Cunningham, C.C. (1975) Parents as therapists and educators. In C.C. Kiernan and F.P. Woodford (eds.) <u>Behaviour Modification with the Severely Retarded</u>. Study Group 8, IRMMH. Amsterdam: Associated Scientific Publishers

Gunstone, C., Hogg, J., Sebba, J., Warner, J. and Almond, S. (1982) <u>Classroom Provision and Organisation for Integrated Preschool Children</u>. Anson House Preschool Project Paper 2. Barkingside: Barnardo's

Hogg, J. (ed.)(1979) <u>Anson House Preschool Project</u>: <u>The First Two Years</u>. Barkingside: Barnardo's

O'Dell, S. (1974) Training parents in behavior modification: a review. <u>Psychological Bulletin</u>, <u>81</u>, 418-433

DISCUSSION

Sally Beveridge drew out for discussion the two major principles which underlie parent-professional partnership in the Anson House Preschool Project:

. that any service provision for young children is best conceived within an ecological framework;
. that partnership between parents and professionals implies parental involvement as members in a multidisciplinary team.

The ecological approach to service provision leads to the recognition that we need to take account of all of a child's relationships and environments in developing our services. First, and most important, we have to consider the most influential setting which is the home and family. This does not mean simply that we should involve the child's parents and family in the intervention that we have designed, but that as far as possible this involvement should be sensitive both to the priorities of needs within the family, and also to the structure of the child and the family's home life. Next, we need to take account of other important influences on the child and family, e.g. paediatric specialists, hospital social workers, health visitors and preschool teachers. It is vital that effective links are established with all professionals who are involved with a family, so that the particular expertise which can be offered by one professional is neither duplicated by nor confounded by the input

of another, and that families do not feel overwhelmed by a multiplicity of information and advice.
    Partnership of parents in a multidisciplinary
team involves a conscious acceptance and valuing of
what parents have to offer and of what they see as
their role as parents. Similarly, it means that we
need to make explicit the roles of all the other
members of the team, by formulating the extent and
boundaries of expertise as well as overlap between
roles. This helps parents to ask pertinent
questions and to learn who can offer which services,
and how to use these services. The aim is that parents will have the ability, the information and most
importantly the confidence to meet and work with a
wide range of professionals in other settings.
    From the detailed questions put to Sally
Beveridge, and to Rita Flanagan the project social
worker, it was clear that the Anson House Preschool
Project aroused a great deal of interest from both
parents and professionals participating in the
seminar. Further description was given of the
stages of careful introduction to the project before
a family decides they want to participate. Thereafter, parents are welcome to attend Anson House as
often as they wish (in addition to the agreed one
session per week) and have the opportunity for contact with other parents in the communal sitting
room; contacts with the other children in the classroom group; and consulting the social worker, who
is always available in the building for individual
advice, group discussion or an informal chat over
coffee. Parents describe this informal contact with
other parents and with the social worker as an invaluable source of support.
    Sally Beveridge also explained further the
composition of the classroom group. The staff endeavour to compose the group of 12 children in such
a way that they represent a developmental continuum,
but this rule is not applied dogmatically. If
possible, any child referred when there is a vacancy
will be taken. The non-handicapped children in the
group may be siblings of the handicapped children,
or may have been referred to the project by a social
worker or health visitor. Often parents of non-
handicapped children refer themselves, having heard
about the project from other parents or contacts
within the community, and wanting their children to
benefit from mixing in an integrated group.
    One further topic of discussion concerned
record-keeping. At Anson House, parents have open
access to the files of their own child. All reports

are written primarily for the parents, who receive the first copy and are asked to correct this if necessary. If the staff receive confidential information from other professionals, they ask for permission to share it with the parents.

Further discussion arose from the observation, expressed particularly by the Dutch and Swedish participants, that parents in Britain seem to be much keener to be involved with professionals than those in other countries. It may be that different approaches work in different places, and that we then need to look at what doesn't suit individuals in each system. Peter Mittler emphasised the need for a range of choice of services. He pointed out the problem that the more professionals find working with parents successful and beneficial to the child, the more they are tempted to produce a model and to try and apply this in every case. Research has shown that generally collaboration between parents and professionals in educational programmes will enhance a child's development. However, collaboration must not be forced on parents: those who want to opt out of partnership with professionals are to be respected in this choice. Generalizations on what is best for families with handicapped children and what they need should be avoided, not only by workers in the field but also on the level of planning of statutory services. In future, we should work towards the individualization of our services and remain very conscious that the element of choice be preserved.

Chapter 7

FATHERS, MOTHERS, SIBLINGS: HOW DO THEY SEE THEMSELVES?

Helen McConachie

As has been described in the previous chapter, the
model of parental involvement developed at the Anson
House Preschool Project is one of partnership and
aims for maximum flexibility. When the parents are
involved in teaching their own children at home, the
approach takes into account individual differences
in parents' interaction styles, and individual
children's particular learning difficulties and
abilities.

On reflection, and in conversation with parents, we become aware of a number of aspects of
bringing up a young child which had not necessarily
been taken account of in the parent teaching work at
Anson House. We lacked consistent information about
the home life of the children attending the project:
how activities fitted into the daily routine, how
much fathers and other children were involved in
child care, what aspects of their child's upbringing
parents saw as the most vital, and so on. Through
the social worker, we would have information about
any problems arising at home, and therefore for any
particular family we could ensure that pressures
were not increased by our expectations of involving
the parent in teaching. However, we wanted to look
beyond the level of 'problems', and to compare
families on more fundamental characteristics. It
seemed very likely that there were differences within and between families of potential relevance to
the degree of success of their involvement in teaching their children.

This chapter concentrates on families of young
children, and on the role of parents as teachers, a
role which parents of mentally handicapped children
are increasingly expected to adopt. However, there
are many varied and shifting interpretations of what
is meant by 'teaching', by 'learning' and by 'parent-

ing'. We may need to consider more throughly what
it is to be a parent of any child, and from that
gain a clearer perspective of how, where and when
teaching may be an appropriate part of a parent's
role.

Many professionals seem to find it easier to
have a model parent in mind - one who sees her or
his handicapped child as a special responsibility
and a special challenge, who gives a lot of individual attention to the child and who is eager and
organised to do special teaching or play sessions.
Yet many parents first and foremost see a little
girl or boy in front of them, a child who wants to
have fun and to play and to be mischievous. They
may expect their child to learn just by being in
different situations and therefore feel that they
are teaching by providing opportunities for the
child. They may feel uncomfortable with a
'didactic' model of parenting or primary concentration on the child as 'handicapped'.

The first section of the chapter will discuss
how parents of young mentally handicapped children
see themselves and their role in bringing up their
children. The following sections explore what is
known about some family members who have received
comparatively little attention - fathers, sisters
and brothers. The basic argument underlying the
discussion is that further progress in developing
services for young mentally handicapped children is
crucially dependent on understanding, and respect-
ing, the range of different ways in which families
think and live their lives. Approaches based merely
on educational technology will fail to meet a
child's or a family's needs, just as institutional
answers failed previously.

HOW PARENTS SEE THEIR ROLE

In talking to parents of young mentally handicapped
children, it is clear that they have a range of
different philosophies both about how to bring up
their children in general, and about how to bring up
their handicapped child. Some see their primary
role as creating a warm, stable environment for the
child; others stress helping the child to learn the
skills required for independence. Some find parent-
hood arduous, others find it enjoyable, and the
feelings may change with different periods of the
child's development. In some countries nowadays,
parents may have been surrounded by exhortation and
advice on playing with their child, from the moment

the handicap is known, through television programmes, popular literature, home visitors, etc.
Some have even been told the unfounded myth that
their child will stop learning at five years old,
and so they must teach everything they can quickly.
The pressure can be quite a burden; it can take the
fun out of playing with the child, and watching his
or her development.

Professional workers need to keep in mind that
parents have a lifelong commitment to their child.
Thus, they are building a relationship and an interaction which will need to change and grow with the
child, and to remain appropriate not only when the
child is very young, but also during the school
years, and eventually when he or she attempts to
establish adult independence.

Most parents want advice on practical handling
of their child, and find positive activitiy one of
the ways in which they come to terms with the
child's handicap. However, advice needs to be based
on a full knowledge of the parents' own ideas and
desires.   There are many difficulties in gathering
such information in a way which does not distort it.
For example, it is unlikely to be a sufficient evaluation to ask parents for their views only at the
end of an intervention programme in which they have
been involved. The statements will be a reaction to
what has been offered, and will not tease out what
else parents might have wanted. If they have been
offered a chance to learn about educational goals
and techniques, they may feel diffident about expressing their own view of their child's needs. One
parent who had been involved in Anson House explained her reaction to involvement in teaching: "A
parent working with a child is not the same as a
teacher teaching. As a parent you are also wanting
to develop other things, for example, exercising
choice; therefore you are not as strict as a
teacher".

In research at Anson House, we have attempted
to explore how parents view bringing up their child,
in a way that will let them speak for themselves,
and yet will also allow for comparisons to be made
between parents, and over time. We will also
attempt to relate parents' views to observed differences in interaction style and to differences or
similarities between fathers and mothers.

Parents were asked to think about a number of
everyday situations which involve themselves and
their children, such as getting the child dressed,
going shopping together, looking at books, etc.

They were then asked to rate each situation on questions such as how enjoyable the situation was for them, how much attention the child required or whether discipline was important to them. The overriding concerns of each parent can be pulled out from the structure of the ratings. For example, one parent saw the most important things for her as being that she and her child should have fun together and communicate well. One situation in which her child insisted on being independent was in playing with toys. It seems likely that conflicts might arise if this parent were involved in a parent teaching programme and was expected to have regular structured sessions with her child (for example, working on shapes or colours). The child might resist working with her; and she might not wish to jeopardize their fun together by being more controlling than usual, even if she agreed with the overall aims of the programme. Another parent grouped together the ideas of teaching, treating the child as 'handicapped' (rather than as normal), and "I get harassed". She seemed enthusiastic about participating in teaching her child, but in subsequent discussion of the ratings realised the ambivalence in her feelings which might have lessened her involvement.

Eliciting parents' ideas about everyday situations can help to identify potential conflicts at the time of offering a teaching course. The process will also begin to establish shared meanings of concepts and will lessen miscommunication between parents and professionals. However, there will be many layers of ideas and concerns not tapped by a concentration on everyday situations. For example, parents look ahead, and worry about how to prepare their children and themselves for the time of entry to school. They may be aware constantly of the conflict between their child's special needs, and how to 'normalise' their own and their child's lives. Professional staff may seem to assume that the central business of life is bringing up children, and to be interested in parents only as members of a special group, 'parents of handicapped children'. Voysey (1975) has suggested there is an implicit official morality of child-rearing and of family life which affects how parents and professionals communicate, and how parents see themselves (eg. "coping splendidly", "self-sacrificing", "just as normal", "changing society's attitudes", etc.). Such complexities may affect crucially the long-term effectiveness of

programmes offered by professionals, if time to
listen and responses to differing family needs are
not built in to the structure of the programme from
the beginning.

FATHERS

Very little has been written specifically about
fathers of handicapped children in comparison with
the voluminous literature on mothers, or about
families, often derived solely from mothers' reports
(McConachie, 1982). Likewise, there has been relatively little research interest in the father's role
in child care, except in relation to the topic of
father-absence. And yet it has long been established that young children may form strong bonds
with several people. Schaffer and Emerson (1964)
showed that relationships with fathers, grandparents
and siblings begin early in life; in about a third
of the infants studied, the primary attachment was
observed and reported to be to the father rather
than to the mother. As roles in child-care have
changed (in Western society), it has become more expected that fathers will be involved in child care.
The extent to which this actually happens remains
unclear; or rather, studies show that mothers are
still responsible for the majority of child care.
Researchers have often used inadequate definitions
of 'father participation'. For example, Newson and
Newson (1968) concluded that 51 per cent of fathers
of four year old children in Nottingham had a 'high
level of participation' in child care. But the only
questions asked were general ones, such as "How much
does your husband have to do with ...?" Fathers
themselves were not interviewed. The answers will
tend to reflect feelings and values rather than
quantitative data. Oakley (1974) gave a more precise definition (though still relative to the rest
of her sample of fathers) and rated only 25 per cent
'highly participant'. The same contrasts in researchers' definitions are apparent in studies of
the families of handicapped children: Hewett (1970)
and Carr (1975) stressed fathers' participation, and
Wilkin (1979) the lack of it.
    In some ways, we might expect the pressures on
fathers of handicapped children to tend to decrease
their involvement. For example, they may feel left
out of the processes of getting and giving information, through being at work during the child's
probably numerous clinic appointments, or visits by
educational home visitors. They have less chance to

128

talk about their feelings and may not easily meet other parents in the same position. They may feel incompetent with this child who is 'different' and so tend to give up. They may feel bitterly disappointed that their ambitions for their child will not be realised.

It certainly would seem desirable to promote consistency in handling the handicapped child, and to help both parents to feel more confident. Yet it would be irresponsible for professionals to issue a blanket exhortation for fathers to be more involved with their handicapped child. It is likely that the primary effect would be to *increase* the burden on mothers, through feeling that it is their failure if the father is not involved. We need more background information on what fathers of handicapped children do at present, so that we can plan any involvement on a sound basis.

I have made a study of children's home routines and of which parent is involved in giving them attention. Nineteen families were involved in the research, each of which included a child who had been identified as developmentally delayed or mentally handicapped, but not multiply handicapped. The children ranged in age between twenty and forty-five months. Parents were interviewed together, and recounted in great detail everything the child had done, and with whom the child had been, for two days including one day when one or both parents had been at work, and one day when they hadn't. Therefore, for many families, the interview took place on a Monday evening. Care was taken to avoid days which had been particularly unusual (e.g. birthdays, illness). Four levels of interaction were defined: 'concentrated', 'continuous', 'available' and 'separate', (cf. Douglas, Lawson, Cooper and Cooper, 1968) and rated for the parents. (Other family members' interaction levels with the child were not established fully.)

In terms of the amount of time each parent was available to the child, fathers' working hours outside the home meant that their weekday time was much less than mothers', except for one unemployed father. However, it was on average over a quarter of the child's day (median 28 per cent, range 1 hr. 30 mins. to 10 hrs. 25 mins. for employed fathers). Thus, fathers were perhaps potentially more available to the children than one commonly thinks is the case.

In research on parent-child interaction it is often noted that the *amount* of time a parent is

129

available may be quite unrelated to the *quality* of
how the time is spent with the child. This observation was confirmed in the present study, in that
the overall amount of time a parent was available to
the child did not predict how much time he or she
spent in 'concentrated' interaction. This level was
rated when parent and child were sharing the activity and giving it their full attention, often with
physical contact involved (e.g. reading books,
dressing). The definition includes the minimum conditions for the kind of structured teaching a parent
might undertake in a programme, though this is not
meant to imply that teaching in any formal sense was
taking place in time so rated. It was observed that
some parents who had relatively little time with the
child spent a large proportion of it in concentrated
interaction, and vice versa. Mothers still overall
had more concentrated interaction than fathers, even
when fathers' lesser time available is taken into
account. On the whole, fathers gave concentrated
attention to the child during play activities and
mothers gave concentrated attention during caretaking activities.

It was striking how widely fathers differed in
the extent of their interaction and involvement with
their children. One reason for this was suggested
by the finding that those fathers who were most involved tended to be the ones whose children could
use words, rather than still being at the stage of
using sounds or gestures. This observation suggests
that fathers may become discouraged, for example,
through not understanding the child's attempts at
communication, rather than not really being interested in playing with the child. Therefore, guidance at the right time might help some fathers to
become more involved with their children early on.

There were clearly differing patterns of co-
operation between parents. As a definition of
'participation in child care', the amount of both
'concentrated' and 'continuous' interaction time was
looked at, therefore including all time when the
parent was at least partly responsible for the
child, and communicating frequently (e.g. mealtimes,
shopping). Of the nineteen families, one father was
the child's primary caretaker, and two more seemed
to take over from the mother at the weekend. Five
couples shared time and responsibility for the child
at the weekend. In eleven families the mother was
always the primary caretaker. Therefore, in some
families it seems an obvious step to involve fathers
as well as mothers in planned programmes. In other

families, we may need to proceed more carefully. The present routine will have its own momentum, which we might threaten by suggesting unrealistic changes. Yet we should keep in mind the potential benefits to both father and mother of fuller information and a more equal sharing of the care of their child.

Once again, flexibility in service provision will be a key factor. Change might begin with case conferences being held in the evenings or in families' homes. Fathers may need professionals to make a special point of their participation being important. For example, they may have perceived their role as beginning when the child is older, and being concerned primarily with discipline and activities outside the home. Yet, with encouragement, they may be able to take time off work to attend particular meetings and workshops. There are cultural differences in how fathers will be involved with professionals. Already, in the case of Asian families, it is often fathers rather than mothers who have detailed contact with services (Beveridge, Flanagan, McConachie and Sebba, 1982). To develop ways in which services can be organised, on a basis of partnership, and sensitive to the needs of all the members of the family, will require imagination and commitment.

BROTHERS AND SISTERS

As well as parents, siblings can often be very significant figures in a young child's life. Studies of the families of mentally handicapped people have tended either to omit or to make only passing reference to the siblings. In the past, parents may have been advised to institutionalize a mentally handicapped child "for the sake of the normal children". However, those studies which are available have drawn a variety of conclusions as to the effects upon brothers and sisters of living with a handicapped child. Some studies have suggested that many siblings feel jealous, embarrassed or aggressive toward the handicapped child (e.g. Kew, 1975) and that older siblings, especially girls, have to undertake a heavy burden of housework (e.g. Gath, 1974). However, the way in which many studies have been conducted have left them difficult to interpret. For example, few studies have actually asked siblings themselves; and few have included a comparison group of siblings whose brother or sister is not handicapped.

When siblings are asked directly, the reported incidence and severity of problems seems low. Relationships with parents, and with the handicapped child, are mostly satisfactory and warm. Grossman (1972) interviewed college-age siblings, and found "a surprising number of brothers and sisters of retarded children who appeared to us to have benefited in some way from the experience of growing up with a handicapped sibling". We asked siblings (aged eight to fifteen years) who were living at home with a younger brother or sister about their everyday activities and attitudes, and found only one aspect which siblings of mentally handicapped children reported significantly more than did a matched group of siblings of non-handicapped children. That was the extent to which the younger child was a disruption, not leaving them alone when they were busy, and tending to wake them up at night. Siblings reported often playing with and helping the younger child and several mentioned buying little presents for him or her. The teenage siblings were rather more negative in their attitudes (whether the child was handicapped or not) and seemed to be reacting as any teenager might to a bothersome younger sister or brother (McConachie and Domb, 1982). It might be suggested that siblings will react more strongly when the handicapped child is older and 'childish' behaviour is less acceptable. However, Gath (1973) did not find any difference in psychological disturbance between those siblings who were born before the handicapped (Down's syndrome) child and those siblings who were born after.

The researchers who have reported a general level of negative reactions in siblings seem to have started with the assumption that there will be harmful effects and so find what they are looking for. Parents, too, may find it difficult to interpret unhappiness or disobedience in a sibling, and may wrongly ascribe its cause to the presence of the handicapped child. They may forget how ordinary it is for siblings to squabble.

In effect, parents often try very hard to make sure that the siblings do not 'lose out' because of the handicapped child. Fuchs (1974) interviewed mothers, and found that many organised the family routine carefully to reduce any potential adverse impact on siblings. For example, they would ensure the handicapped child did not interfere with home work. She found six (out of twenty-five) families which did not have deliberate organisation and in five of these tension was noted between the siblings and the handicapped child. Thus it is important not just to look at siblings in isolation but to study the family system and routines in order to elucidate how they are currently balanced to favour all the children in the family.

Background information of this type would seem essential in considering whether or not siblings could be drawn into programmes to help the young child. There are few reports of sibling groups in the literature. Weinrott (1974) described a summer training camp for teenage siblings, where they followed a behaviour modification course, and then applied their new knowledge at home with the mentally handicapped member of the family. The aim of the programme was not that siblings should spend more time concentrating on the handicapped child but that the time that they already did spend should be as helpful as possible. Therefore, the siblings learned strategies for minimizing disruptive incidents and ways to help their brothers or sisters to become more independent. Hart and Walters (1981) have described a British workshop for siblings which also included information on behaviour management and teaching skills. Other sibling groups meet in Liverpool and in Swansea, and a newsletter for siblings ('*Sibs*') started in 1980.

However, given the research findings outlined above, it would seem that any aim to provide services, such as therapeutic discussion groups, for all siblings would be misplaced. It is undoubtedly true that some siblings find living with a handicapped child hard (as, for example, Fairbrother (1980) described in welcoming *Sibs* newsletter). We need to look in greater depth at what difficulties these siblings have faced, and what help they might welcome. Those who do want to take part in activities connected with their mentally handicapped sister or brother possibly will gain most from goal-directed activities, such as teaching new skills, acting as advocates for their brother or sister or participating in their own siblings' organisations.

CONCLUSIONS

In this chapter a number of themes have been outlined of relevance to families' involvement in programmes for young mentally handicapped children. The child's activities and routines at home require consideration in order to ensure generalization and maintenance of new learning. It is suggested that programmes which respect the current organization at home will be more successfully taken up than those which unwittingly demand changes in routine or ignore current family structures of child-care. Likewise, parents have views on bringing up children which are not happened on by chance, but have been worked out through considerable experience. Professional workers need to keep in mind that they can potentially do harm as well as good in intervening with a family.

All this is not to say that we just need to leave things to families' good sense. A handicapped child does have special needs and parents usually do ask for practical guidance. But there is a need for flexibility in responding to an individual family's current viewpoint and practices if parental involvement is to be a real partnership.

There are many difficulties to be overcome in making partnership a reality. Professional workers do not necessarily adjust well to being 'equal partners'. It is often still the case that parents are told what the child's programme should be, without involvement in decision making, even if they are to be the main agents of carrying out the programme. Once a programme has been entered into by parents, they may feel they have no alternative but to drop out, if it fails to take account of their present situation. For example, a service geared to practical teaching might not offer the time and sensitivity to talk through complex emotions or overriding practical difficulties at home. No one type of service, be it a home advisory service, a toy library, a parent workshop or an integrated nursery, is able to meet the needs of all families. The important thing is not the invention of new structures of services but rather flexibility in responding to each individual family over time. And that requires professionals to really listen to parents and siblings. Partnership remains the goal to guide our efforts.

REFERENCES

Beveridge, S., Flanagan, R., McConachie, H. and
    Sebba, J. (1982) Parental Involvement in Anson
    House. Anson House Preschool Project Paper 3.
    Barkingside: Barnardo's
Carr, J. (1975) Young Children with Down's Syndrome.
    London: Butterworth
Douglas, J.W.B., Lawson, A., Cooper, J.E. & Cooper,
    E. (1968) Family interaction and the activities of young children. Journal of Child

Psychology and Psychiatry, 9, 157-171

Fairbrother, P. (1980) Siblings. _Parents' Voice_, 30, 22

Fuchs, J. (1974) The impact of mentally handicapped children on family routine, with particular reference to siblings. Unpublished Masters Thesis, University of London

Gath, A. (1973) The school age siblings of mongol children. _British Journal of Psychiatry_, 123, 161-167

Gath, A. (1974) Sibling reactions to mental handicap: a comparison of the brothers and sisters of mongol children, _Journal of Child Psychology and Psychiatry_, 15, 187-198

Grossman, F.K. (1972) _Brothers and Sisters of Retarded Children: an Exploratory Study_. New York: Syracuse University Press

Hart, D. and Walters, J. (1981) A group work project with siblings of mentally handicapped children. _Association for Child Psychology and Psychiatry News_, no. 8, 6-9

Hewett, S. (1970) _The Family and the Handicapped Child_. London: Allen and Unwin

Kew, S. (1975) _Handicap and Family Crisis_. London: Pitman Press

McConachie, H. (1982) Fathers of mentally handicapped children. In N. Beail and J. McGuire (eds.) _Fathers: Psychological Perspectives_. London: Junction Books

McConachie, H. and Domb, H. (1982) An interview study of the siblings of mentally handicapped children. Unpublished manuscript, Hester Adrian Research Centre, Manchester

Newson, J. & Newson, E. (1968) _Four Years Old in an Urban Community_. London: Allen and Unwin

Oakley, A. (1974) _The Sociology of Housework_. London: Robertson

Schaffer, H.R. & Emerson, P.E. (1964) The development of social attachments in infancy. _Monographs of the Society for Research in Child Development_, 29 (3, Serial no. 94)

Voysey, M. (1975) _A Constant Burden: The Reconstitution of Family Life_. London: Routledge and Kegan Paul

Weinrott, M. (1974) A training program in behavior modification for siblings of the retarded. _American Journal of Orthopsychiatry_, 44, 362-375

Wilkin, D. (1979) _Caring for the Mentally Handicapped Child_. London: Croom Helm

135

DISCUSSION

In introducing her paper, Helen McConachie raised
the question of the purposes of conducting research
into the relationship between parents and professionals. Two considerations had informed the theme
of her paper. Firstly, she stressed that we need to
be careful of what we mean by the word 'family'.
Very often the word has been used loosely and has
meant, both for services and research, simply
'mother'. In order to take account of how a child
experiences the world, we need to focus on what
actually happens at home, rather than what we supp-
ose to happen or what happens in a clinic or school.
    Secondly, she emphasised that adequate evalu-
ation of early intervention must include more sensitive criteria than numbers of children seen, or
numbers of skills gained on a checklist. We must
take account of long term outcomes and of less
easily quantifiable factors such as parents' confidence, and the level of stress in family life.
    Because of these two considerations, her paper
had included more in the way of description of
research methods and an outline of some research
results than did most of the other papers. She
wanted to demonstrate that it may be possible to
quantify aspects of family life and parents' per-
ceptions of bringing up children, in ways which do
not unduly constrain and distort what actually
happens. Collection of this type of objective and
complex information should precede the design of
a structure for collaboration between parents and
professionals.
    Mariet van Hattum from the Netherlands had pre-
pared a detailed consideration of the themes of the
paper. She agreed with the observation that not all
parents will want to work with their child as a
'teacher'. The relationship between parent and
child differs fundamentally from the relationship
between a teacher and child: for one thing, it is
lifelong. Children occupy a central place in a
teacher's work, and the teacher has chosen to do
this job. However, should we take for granted that
the child will have a central place in the parents'
life? And parents have not chosen to have a handicapped child. Notwithstanding the respect paid to
parents' life-styles and wishes in the paper, it
gave the impression of professionals' standards pre-
dominating.
    Similarly, in considering siblings, profession-
als will often seem to focus on the handicapped

child as the centre of the family. A brief interview will not be able to bring out the character of the complex ways in which siblings may feel. Where siblings suffer, it may be that they suffer especially because of their parents' sadness and overburdening, and not directly because of the handicapped child. Also, the ambivalence which all parents feel about their children may be divided in a family with a handicapped child. The handicapped child may cause much stress, and the other children be seen as easy, or feel they should not cause any trouble. On the other hand, a handicapped child's passivity may be seen as easy, and the normally vital child seen as a nuisance.

We can regard it as very positive when siblings want to be involved in caring for their handicapped brother or sister. But it also has a dangerous side to it. The siblings have experiences and opportunities open to them which the handicapped child does not have, and they may feel 'survivors' guilt' because of this. Often siblings enter careers connected with caring for handicapped people. But does this choice really suit their personality, or do they single out this occupation in order not to feel a burden of guilt?

In general discussion, the consensus seemed to be that siblings may be prevented from having problems if other parents and professionals succeed in making their parents aware that the normally developing children are just as important as the mentally handicapped child and that they should be careful not to give them a feeling of being left out.

Cliff Cunningham raised the question of whether we can perhaps create problems by looking for them. How much should we prepare people for possible problems? The dilemma for professionals may be whether to offer help, information and counselling, or to wait until parents ask for it. The discussion again highlighted the notion that the needs of families with a mentally handicapped member change over time. From the very beginning families should have access to help, either statutory or voluntary, in a flexible system which enables them to utilize these resources if and whenever they choose to do so.

SECTION FOUR: THE SCHOOL YEARS

Chapter 8

COLLABORATION BETWEEN PARENTS AND TEACHERS OF SCHOOL-AGE CHILDREN

Barbara Smith

> ....the successful education of children
> with special educational needs is dependent
> upon the full involvement of their parents
>
> Warnock (1978)

The insistence that parental involvement is a vital
component in the educative process if handicapped
children are to develop to their fullest potential
is at the heart of the Report "Special Educational
Needs" prepared by the Warnock Committee on educational provision for all handicapped children. Such
involvement is referred to as a partnership between
parents and professionals. It is this concept of
partnership to which I am utterly committed in my
dual role, both as mother of a severely mentally
handicapped adolescent son and as a teacher of mentally handicapped pupils at an ESNS school.

Just over ten years ago it would have been surprising if parents of mentally handicapped children
in this country realised that there was a contribution they could make to furthering their children's educational development, for our society did-
not consider them to be educable. Prior to the Education (Handicapped Children) Act 1970, those children ascertained as mentally handicapped were segregated from the educational system. As a parent, I
received a formal letter from my local education
committee before my son's fifth birthday telling me
that he was "suffering from such a disability of
mind as to make him unsuitable from education at
school" and that the decision would be recorded,
after which it wouldn't be possible for him to be
admitted to any school in the authority or be sent
to any other school. However, April 1971 saw the
transfer of responsibility for mentally handicapped

children to the Education Service, with some 24,000 children in Junior Training Centres, 8,000 children then in hospitals and an uncertain number at home or in private institutions at last entitled to receive special education.

It was at this time that Cunningham and Jeffree undertook their first two pioneer workshops with highly motivated, self-selected groups of parents of young children, and showed that active involvement of parents in the education of their mentally handicapped children was both feasible and fruitful (Cunningham and Jeffree, 1971, 1975). These workshops must be of historical significance in the development of parental involvement and have been followed by many others in different parts of the country.

What follows aims to be a fairly comprehensive yet brief overview of current practice in collaboration between parents and teachers of school-age children, from which models for future development may be drawn.

AN A - Z OF PARENT/TEACHER COLLABORATION

A̲   ASSESSMENT

Differing types of assessment take place throughout the school-life of a mentally handicapped child. These may occur formally or informally.

1.   Assessment along with discovery and diagnosis are contributing stages of the three-fold process whereby a child is 'ascertained' as being in need of special educational treatment and upon which subsequent school placement is based. Up to now, the necessary paperwork procedure (S.E. forms) has not allowed for the parents to give any written statement about their child's needs, although an Educational Psychologist or previous Head Teacher may incorporate this. As a result of the 1981 Education Act new procedures are being introduced which will give parents a somewhat greater share in assessment.

2.   On-going educational assessment should be the basis for curriculum planning in school and, some would argue, for the total management of the child. This may be undertaken by the school without reference to the parents or may be a joint undertaking.

I myself have had experience as a teacher of older pupils in working with their parents in the joint completion of the *Pathways to Independence*

Checklists compiled by Jeffree and Cheseldine (1982). The parents and I have then jointly agreed suitable curriculum objectives based on emergent strengths and weaknesses which we have considered to have particular relevance.

3. Assessments by visiting specialists or professional workers may concern the general condition of the child, specific sensory defects or behavioural problems. Some schools invite parents into the school for every such assessment, whether routine or otherwise, believing it to be the right of parents to have the opportunity to attend, whereas other schools may only invite parents in for selected assessments.

4. Assessment relating to the post-school placement of all young people will occur towards the end of their special schooldays and will usually involve the pupil and parent and a number of other interested professional workers (eg. careers officer, educational psychologist, doctor, social worker and teacher), as aspirations and abilities are considered in relation to possible placement. In my experience, this assessment is a real point of interest amongst parents; their involvement is vital in promoting successful transition from school to post-school life.

B   BOOKLET

Increasing numbers of special schools are producing a booklet about the school. In many cases this is specifically produced for parents and prospective parents. It may include illustrations and will give basic information which may be of a very practical nature but may also include details relating to the aims and organisation of the school and curriculum content.

C   CASE CONFERENCES

These are normally formal meetings called for a specific reason to enable a number of people working with a child or young person to share assessments and experiences and to make treatment and placement recommendations. Parents may or may not be invited to the case conferences depending on the reason for which they are called.

In my experience it is customary for inclusion of parents to be the norm - except when there has been a very specific reason for exclusion.

D   DIARIES

Diaries or home-school notebooks exist in a great
many schools for the purpose of written communication between home and school. In some schools
they travel to and from home daily, either in the
charge of the pupils (who may be trained to accept
that responsibility) or in the care of a transport
escort who accompanies the children. In other
schools the book may be sent on a more intermittent
basis.
     In my experience diaries seem to be used in
three ways: for general items of information (eg.
"Hello, my name's Barbara Smith and I'm the new
teacher.."); for more specific instruction (eg."...
his calipers seem to be rubbing his leg, will you
look at them in school today and see what you
think?"); and for active collaboration on a joint
teaching venture (eg. in a programme on undressing
skills, a parental comment one morning was, "Only
help last night was shoe-lace, which she pulled into
knot, and unfastening her bra - the other's not like
that, she can do it herself. I'll get her another
like that one then she'll be able to manage it on
her own all the time.").

E   EQUIPMENT

Equipment in the form of books, toys and specific
teaching material may be sent home on a daily or
longer term basis. This may be selected by pupil,
parent or teacher and may be for a very general
reason (eg. pupil may choose a favourite toy or
book) or for a very specific reason (eg. "4 sets of
that word lotto game, so that the whole family can
play together with him after tea.").
     I have found it necessary to make very careful
selection of equipment to ensure that vital classroom materials are available when needed in school.
As pupils have proved their reliability to return
things daily and without damage, so they have progressed to the more 'vital' things. I have found
that the use of a clearly marked bag travelling
daily between home and school has enabled this
borrowing facility to be extended to younger or more
severely handicapped children.

F   FORMAL RECORDING SYSTEM

Most schools have some formal system for recording
documentation about pupils. Frequently the infor-

144

mation involved falls into one of two categories, either that which results from professional consultation and may be of a sensitive nature and passed in confidence, and that which is of a more factual nature, relating to the child, and family, progress and attendance. In my experience the former information has been on restricted access, whereas the second type of recording has usually been readily available for parents and all professionals working with the child.

There would appear to be some quite distinctive methods of recording this second type of information. Some schools use a tick chart system, some a termly or yearly record book in which they note progress. Other establishments, however, use a more comprehensive record showing details of assessments, current objectives and evaluation. My own records have tended to be of the latter kind and I have made use of them with parents in discussion about their child's work and progress.

It is my personal belief that all documentation about pupils should be available to their parents and that this would aid contributors, from whatever discipline, in their pursuit of objectivity with such reports.

G   GOVERNORS

The inclusion of parents on to the Governing Bodies of schools is relatively new in some areas and is by no means accepted universally as yet. Some consider that parent governors represent a formal means of collective co-operation between parents and school.

H   HOMEWORK

Homework activities can provide a useful means of joint involvement and may occur for a number of different reasons.

1.   They may relate to a joint teaching programme (eg. in an agreed pre-writing programme, a pupil is closely supervised by a parent at home going over lightly pencilled motor patterns with a felt tip marker).

2.   They may relate to the request of a parent or suggestion from the teacher to give the child a useful activity at home - eg. a pupil living in high-rise flats in an inner city area, and who goes out from home very rarely, was given a holiday workbook compiled by the teacher for her to

use over the holidays. Not only was all the work
completed but the family had found the activity so
useful that further work was prepared by a brother.
   3.   Finally, it may be that pupils want to
take home a homework book or activity because they
are aware that there are others doing such a thing
and want to be like them.

I   INFORMATION

Basic information will include notification of
school openings and closures for the year, general
letters from the Head Teacher relating to special
events or changes at the school. This kind of information may not be individually addressed but may
be given to transport escorts to give to each
parent. However, such a system might run into
difficulties unless very tightly organised by the
school to ensure a system of cover for children who
are absent or who are not met by a parent from the
transport. A second form of information is that
which is personally addressed and may include a
child's annual report or personal letter to a
Parent-Teacher Association Committee member. It
seems that this type of information is not 'at risk'
in the same way.

J   JOINT INVOLVEMENT

The joint involvement of parents and professionals
will vary considerably in the level of intensity.
   1.   At a general level there will be those
parents who have some knowledge of their child's
progress and what is going on rather generally in
school and are keen to co-operate in a simple
venture. For example, when it was known that we
were involved in watching the series of "Let's Go"
TV programmes for mentally handicapped young people
and adults, one father watched the repeat programmes
at home with his child and the series gave rise to
some useful communication.
   2.   At a more intense level will be the joint
involvement where parent and teacher have agreed
together a suitable target, have developed some
breakdown into steps of the target behaviour, work
with the child towards it, and exchange information
regarding progress. For example, such a programme
arose in the case of an eleven year old pupil of
mine who was having great problems in fastening his
rather small coat! After collaboration between his
mum and myself, the proposed new coat was bought

146

with a specially selected large zip. A joint
teaching programme was evolved, using a backward-
training procedure, and the pupil managed to un-
fasten the zip within twenty-four hours and to
fasten it in just under a week.

3.   There will be those parents who do not
wish to engage in any form of joint involvement
with the school. I believe that this is a right
which parents have and which should be recognised
by professionals.

K   KITCHEN FACILITIES
–

The availability of some form of kitchen facilities
(ie. independent provision for making a drink and
washing up) along with a parents' room to act as an
informal meeting place or 'parents' den' is a relatively new innovation. However, some schools are
providing such a facility if space permits.

It is my belief that for parents to have their
own base in school is of the utmost importance, as
long as they know that they do still have easy
access to the classrooms and teachers.

L   LEND-A-HAND
–

The 'lend-a-hand' involvement of parents has been
continuing in many schools for a long time. In
this venture parents may volunteer their services
or expertise in order to help the school.

In my own experience, I have found it most
valuable to have regular parent volunteers to help
with weekly riding sessions, to have a fathers'
working party make or repair items of equipment,
and to have parents with specific expertise who
have shared this by working in with the pupils.

M   MEETINGS
–

Meetings in schools have occurred for many years.
They often fall into one of two categories: those
which are for all parents (eg. an informative
evening when the welfare rights officer comes and
is willing to answer questions) and those which are
'class' meetings where parents whose children are
all in the same class are invited into school together to meet with one another and the class
teacher in an informal way or for a specific
purpose (eg. to hear about short term care facilities from the Senior Social Worker responsible).

N   NEEDS OF PARENTS

That collaborative ventures should arise from an
awareness of the needs of parents is a fundamental
principle. Warnock (1978) sees these as being
three-fold, the need for information, advice and
practical help. That of *information* relates to diagnosis, prognosis and the availability of services;
that of *advice* is considered by many to be the two-
way process in conjunction with the professional
which encourages the parent to play a fuller role
in the child's education; that of *practical help*
relates to the acquisition of allowances, aids and
relief (through use of formalised or informal care
facilities).

O   OPENING EVENING OR DAYS

The Open Evening or Open Day would seem to be quite
a tradition in many special schools. In some cases,
it provides little more than the opportunity for
parents to walk round the school, note the attract-
ive displays and have a chat with staff. However,
there are those where it is held shortly after reports have been sent out to parents, and it is held
specifically to afford parents the formal opportunity of coming into school to discuss their
children's work and progress with the class teacher
and visiting specialists.

P   PARENT-TEACHER ASSOCIATION

Attitudes toward Parent-Teacher Associations tend
to be polarised. Some decry them completely whilst
others consider them to be a vital part of school
life. The objectives of such associations may vary,
although most seem to draw their activities from
fund-raising, social or informative events. In my
own experience, I feel that much valuable contact
has been encouraged through parents and professionals working together in the organisation and
running of family social events where teachers are
clearly not perceived as the experts.

Q   QUESTIONNAIRES

There are some schools where due consideration is
given to the views of parents in relation to the
school curriculum and joint involvement. The information is gathered by means of the school send-
ing out a questionnaire to the parents who are then

148

asked to complete it.

Recently I have had experience of such involvement. Seventy five per cent of parents completed the questionnaire. When asked about their aims for their children, Self Help Skills were thought to be very important, closely followed by Language and Communication (both with ratings of over 80 per cent). Independence came next, closely followed by Appropriate Behaviours (both with ratings of over 60 per cent). In relation to advice, 75 per cent of parents who completed the questionnaires wanted advice and 44 per cent wanted specific advice. Of those who wanted advice, 44 per cent said they would like it given at home, 12 per cent said definitely not at home, 30 per cent said they would like it at school, 14 per cent said definitely not at school; however, the most requested method for advice was the Diary or Home-School Notebook with 56 per cent asking for this and only 10 per cent not wanting it. Of those who wanted advice in school, twice as many as those who said they would like to be involved in a workshop approach said they would like to receive individual advice.

Such findings were valuable for a number of reasons: firstly, it was rewarding to the school staff to have such a high proportion of questionnaires returned, and secondly, the responses helped the school in determining its future parental involvement policy and in staff discussions relating to curriculum priority areas.

R   REPORTS

It would seem that most schools record the progress of their children at least on a yearly basis. An increasing number of schools now send out annual reports to parents. In some cases this is then followed by an opportunity for dialogue. I believe it is the right of every parent to receive an annual report and consider that any schools not providing parents with one are failing in their responsibility.

S   SENIOR PUPILS' PARENTS' GROUP

Some schools have been aware of the problems faced by senior pupils in their transition from school to post-school life, but there has been an increasing awareness of the parents' role in this transition and of their preparation for it.

A social worker and I have been jointly res-

ponsible for the formation and running of a Senior
Pupils' Parents' Group where post-school opportunities have been investigated by means of talks
(some illustrated), discussions and visits. Experts
were invited to give information, and subsequently
the relevance and application to individual needs
were considered and developed more informally.

T TELEPHONE CONTACT

Telephone contact, where parents have a 'phone, may
be used either to supplement or take the place of
home-school diaries.
    I have found this approach to be most valuable
where parents are not fully literate, but have also
used it to give support and encouragement relating
to joint programme implementation. There have been
rare occasions when I have felt my right to privacy
has been impinged upon once a parent knows my
'phone number. However, as a parent, I have
greatly valued being able to relieve my own son's
frustration at his inability to communicate something 'vital' about his day at school by a short
'phone call to his teacher.

U USEFUL LITERATURE

Leaflets and booklets relating to local provision
of services and welfare rights for the handicapped
are made available to parents in some schools. The
parents' den, if provided, is an obvious place for
these to be displayed, along with any books that
are specifically written for parents.

V VISITS

Parents' visits into school have been encountered
for many years but of more recent origin is the
visiting of teachers to see parents of their pupils
in their own home, either in the daytime or evening.
The visit of parents into school may be at a pre-
arranged time for a specific purpose, but many feel
it important for parents to have informal access to
the school at any time. Such access may pose problems for both parents and teachers alike. The
teachers may not be able to make themselves available at short notice, and the parents might have to
be left waiting about, unless there is a parents'
den where they can feel at home.

<u>W</u>   WORKSHOPS

A number of schools have used developments of the
workshop model pioneered by Cunningham and Jeffree
(1975) as a means of joint collaboration, with
parents being helped to assess their children's
abilities, select learning objectives, break these
down into steps, work with their children and evaluate progress. In some cases other professionals
(eg. psychologists and speech therapists) have co-
llaborated with school staff in such ventures.
     In working with parents of older children, I
have adapted the workshop model and tend to use the
principles on a much more individualistic and informal basis although I believe that the topic 'Use
of Leisure' could well prove to be of interest to
enough parents of older pupils to make a more traditional workshop viable.
     I have known one teacher of profoundly handi-
capped children helping his parents increase their
effectiveness by putting volunteers through a
shortened course in behaviour modification based on
a course he had himself undertaken.

<u>X</u>   XMAS ACTIVITIES

Xmas activities (eg. Nativity play, pantomime or
concert), Harvest Services, Sports Days and other
social events are held in many schools and seem to
be important to a wide range of parents who appear
to enjoy the participation of their children in
these more 'normal' school events.

<u>Y</u>   YOUTH ACTIVITIES

Some schools run regular Youth Clubs for their
pupils and may involve parents in helping with this
activity. Others may run a Duke of Edinburgh Award
Scheme where collaboration with parents is an important factor. Another vital "youth activity" has
been the occasional 'minding service' arranged in
school for pupils whose parents are then able to
attend some school function.

<u>Z</u>   ZEAL

Success or failure of collaboration may well be related to the extent of the ZEAL (hearty and per-
sistent endeavours) of professionals for parental
involvement!

REFERENCES

Cunningham, C.C. and Jeffree, D.M. (1971) Working with Parents: Developing a Workshop Course for Parents of Young Mentally Handicapped Children. Manchester: National Society for Mentally Handicapped Children (N.W. Region)

Cunningham, C.C. and Jeffree, D.M. (1975) The organisation and structure of workshops for parents of mentally handicapped children. Bulletin of the British Psychological Society, 28, 405-411

Jeffree, D.M. and Cheseldine, S. (1982) Pathways to Independence. Sevenoaks, Kent: Hodder and Stoughton

Warnock, H.M. (1978) Special Educational Needs. Report of the Committee of Enquiry into the Education of Handicapped Children and Young People. Cmnd. 7212. London: HMSO

Chapter 9

"HANDICAPPED CHILD - TAXI"

Shirley Rheubottom

A taxi or bus service to school is one of the more
mundane and simple measures of support for parents
of handicapped children given by local authorities,
but has broader implications for families and consequences far beyond giving relief and help with
transport. What is very important for parents is
how the taxi service affects the kind of involvement
in the school and in their child's education that
would be expected, routine and unquestioned, from a
parent of an ordinary young child. The threat of
losing this involvement has highlighted its importance for some parents and brought into focus the
reasons they wish to collect and fetch their child
from school. These reasons will be explored below
and consideration will be given to ways in which a
transport service can be modified or made more
flexible to take them into account, as well as ways
in which other forms of parent involvement could
compensate.

THE RESEARCH INTERVIEWS

This chapter arises from a series of ethnographic
interviews with parents of children who have at one
time attended the Anson House Preschool Project and
have now entered state schools full time. By way
of introduction, I shall discuss a few selective
aspects of ethnographic interviewing, a methodolog-
ical tool widely used in sociological and social
anthropological research. It should be noted that
ethnographic interviewing has many things in common
with other forms of interviewing, i.e. those known
as in-depth, thematic, conversational, psycho-
analytic, counselling and non-directive interviews,
to give a few examples. However, I shall point out
some of the distinctive features of the ethnographic

interview. More detailed accounts can be found in Paul (1953) and Spradley (1979).

First and foremost the ethnographic interview is a strategy for getting people to talk about what they know. It is an attempt to understand how other people see their experience and to obtain a description of it from their point of view. Ethnography means learning from people and that to learn from people, one must be taught by them; consequently, the researcher must become the student. It is assumed that the researcher has a naive ignorance about what the informant (parent) knows and has experienced. The researcher asks very brief orienting questions, which may be asked over and over in slightly different contexts with frequent requests for clarification, e.g. "tell me about...", "describe...", "what is the difference between...", "give me an example...". The parent talks about activities and events that make up his or her lifestyle and by doing so defines what is important for the researcher to find out. The principle that the researcher is there to learn guides the questioning within the limits of the focus of the research. In the ethnographic interview, the parent teaches the researcher and thence a wider audience. This gives dignity, respect and importance to what the parent has to say: the parent becomes the expert.

The ethnographic interview, unlike ordinary conversation, is very one-sided, i.e., the informant does most of the talking. The researcher limits her or himself primarily to questions or statements to guide the parent, and then comments or makes re-statements to encourage the informant to continue, to give some approval for the direction being taken, and to indicate attentiveness and interest as well as placing value on what is being said. This approach could as easily be used to establish the view of professionals or of one professional group about another. It happens that in this paper the view of the parents focussed on educational officials. It must be recognized that while professionals' views are often heard and represented, it is relatively rarely that the position of parents is presented from their point of view. Frequently, professionals have presented what parents' roles and contributions ought to be within the conceptual framework of their own disciplines and professional outlook.

MAKING THE CHILD DIFFERENT

Parents have reported that they are informed by
school officials or by the educational psychologist
that their handicapped child will be collected in a
taxi when the child reaches school intake age and is
offered a place in some form of Local Authority
special provision. Some Local Authorities are more
assertive than others in insisting or implying that
all children use the transport service. For many
parents, this assistance is most appreciated since
it relieves some stress and strain and creates no
additional problems for the family. For others, who
may also welcome this assistance, it has broader implications which are not so positive and far out-
weigh any benefits.

One such implication is that parents who aspire
to having their child treated in as many ways as
possible as any ordinary child find that using a
taxi service is another means of differentiating
their child and family from the norm. This differ-
entiation - some prefer to call it discrimination -
extends to the family, the neighbourhood and the
school. This is especially so for children who are
moderately handicapped, have non-handicapped siblings, and whose placements may be in diagnostic
units or special ESNM units attached to ordinary infant schools. In addition many parents have, up to
this point in the child's life, been able to arrange
for a place in an ordinary playgroup. They report
the influence these experiences have had on their
expectations and hopes for finding other integrated
settings for their child.

An illustrative case was reported by a parent
whose handicapped child attends a special unit in
the same infant school where her non-handicapped
sibling attends a nursery class. These parents had
been planning to take both children to school in the
family car. One of the reasons for selecting this
school was that it was nearby and it would be feasible for both parents to share this responsibility.
However, when admission to the school was settled,
they were surprised to find out that :

> They just assumed, well the psychologist
> assumed that Dorothy would go in the taxi, so
> she would be like the other children in the
> unit - not like the other children in the
> school - the other children in the unit.

This special unit is attached to an ordinary infant
school for the explicit purpose of promoting the
integrated education of handicapped children.
Before rejecting the taxi service, the parents tried
to effect a compromise whereby the non-handicapped
sibling could ride in the taxi as well.

> We have never been able to get John in
> officially....He goes to the same school now
> and they wouldn't give him a place in the
> taxi.

But conditions for financial support restrict use of
the taxi to handicapped children. Therefore, the
handicapped child was being set apart not only from
other children in the school but also from other
children in the family. Previously these two children had both attended an integrated nursery classroom, and would have continued to go to school together if both were non-handicapped. The parents
were concerned that the handicapped child should
develop and maintain ties and friendships with other
children in the neighbourhood and school. Although
they could appreciate the teacher's rationale for
wishing the handicapped child to have an informal
opportunity to associate and develop friendships
with the children in the unit, they were equally
concerned about her exclusive association, or "being
lumped together", with other children who had behaviour problems or were handicapped. In the first instance, the use of the taxi interfered unnecessarily
with the relationship with the sibling as they
wished it to develop, and in the second it pushed
the handicapped child into an additional segregated
setting for other than academic reasons. In fact,
it would deprive her of an integrated experience
well within her capacity to manage.
    The parent explained how this differentiation
extended into the family in another way. Parents
were expected to collect and fetch the non-handicapped child, but were unable to do the same with
the handicapped child if the taxi were used. As the
mother put it:

> Then there was no provision for me to go in
> the taxi because there was no way that they
> could bring me home.

Thus it prevented them having the same kind of informal contact with their handicapped child's
teacher that they had with their non-handicapped

child's teacher. This leads to a chain of events
which could unwittingly contribute to the isolation
of the family from the handicapped child and the
child from the family, a division contrary to
current trends toward integration and community-
based care.

Another example was reported by a parent whose
friend had a handicapped child attending a special
school.

> ...but there again as my friend pointed out,
> she drove her other child to school and it was
> the same journey more or less, so why couldn't
> she drive Gordon to school? Because a normal
> child you would have taken to school, you
> wouldn't put on a bus. The only place where
> he was actually being different in normal
> everyday life would have been if he had been
> put on the bus. It made him different from
> other children in this neighbourhood. Whereas
> if he went to school in the car he was just
> the same as all the other children.

Again the effect is that the child is made different, quite unnecessarily, from his or her own
family and neighbourhood.

Labelling is a problem which parents face
regularly especially with children whose medical
diagnosis is Down's syndrome and whose physical
features reflect this. This is a problem they meet
in the school and in the community, and one which
using the taxi service exacerbates. More importantly, however, is how the use of a taxi service
labels a child within the family, and brings the
family to discriminate against one of its own
members - the handicapped child.

One parent described how the educational
psychologist made a concerted effort to 'wean' her
child from her by asking the child's teacher to see
to it:

> ...that Mrs. Bales lets the child go by taxi,
> she shouldn't take her to school by car.

To which the teacher responded:

> Look, what is wrong with taking a child to
> school by car? I took my child to school
> until she was eleven or twelve.

Earlier the parent had told the psychologist:

No, she won't go by taxi...I shall expect to
take her...I feel it is perfectly reasonable
to take a five year old to school. Why should
she go by taxi?

The parent in anger summed up her view of this
episode:

Handicapped child equals taxi!

INTERACTION BETWEEN PARENTS AND TEACHERS

While the issue of integration was not of central
concern to all families interviewed (irrespective of
the nature or degree of the child's handicap), informal interaction with the teacher was of general
concern. It is easy to have this kind of contact
while collecting and fetching the child; in cases
where the child does go by taxi, some parents and
teachers have found other means of achieving regular
informal contact, e.g. the telephone, school-home
notebooks, escorts, and invitations to come at any
time to the school. They emphasize communication is
the key to this informal interaction with the
teacher. Often the communication centres on information about the child's physical needs, e.g. feeding, toileting, sleep and also general mood. But
these exchanges also extend to academic skills which
traditionally have been the exclusive domain of
educationalists. Exchanging information on items of
mutual concern, not exclusively the domain of either
parents or teachers, provides continuity from one
setting to another, i.e. from home to school and
back home again.

And you know I'd go and they would say he has
had two dinners today, you know, roast beef
and Yorkshire pudding...that was a big problem with Paul, his eating, and I got very
full reports on what he had or had not had.

The problem of communication not only applies
to children living at home but also to those attending residential schools who return home at holidays.
In one instance the Local Education Authority would
have paid for a taxi, driver and escort for a full
day to make the 400 miles round trip. The parent
refused the offer, accepting petrol money instead
and arranging for a friend to accompany her. Since
the Local Authority paid for escort and driver only
when they had to provide transport, it saved them a

substantial sum. The parent was aware how tiring and inconvenient the trip was for her and what additional strains it put on the family, but explained its importance:

> I felt if I go down to the school, you can talk to the teachers yourself and the people there and find out what is going on. And they'll say what they are up to and what they are doing with Pauline. So that when she comes home I can try and keep her more or less in the same routine.

When returning after the holiday respite at home, she described her discussion with the staff:

> Usually when I get down, I'll say, oh she did this or she didn't do that. She's been dirty or she's been a little devil this time or she's been playing up or...she actually stayed dry all night...I usually tell them anything that she's done that she doesn't usually do. And of course we tell them the funny incidents...it will remind them of something that she's done while she's been there and they say, "yes," and so we get the feedback that way.

It is possible that while this exchange may have little to do with formal education or parent involvement, it assumes greater importance when a child is away from home for substantial periods of time. It validates the parent's earlier decision to place the child in a residential setting. This parent was reassured by what she saw.

> You walk in there and there is an atmosphere in the house...now it doesn't matter how many of the children are in...it is so nice to just sit there. You feel so relaxed. It is so calming...I think many a time then, "It's no wonder Pauline does so well for them because there is no rigid atmosphere."

Contact appears to be critical in the transition period from being at home to starting school for the first time. Parents seek continuity generally, but probably more so with a handicapped child who is often more dependent upon an adult. The child may also be less able to communicate his or her own needs or what has happened during the day. As one parent expressed it:

> I actually took her the first day...with
> another mum in the taxi. We both took them
> there and settled them down...you feel a bit
> more confident you know, just taking them
> that first day.

This parent continued to have daily communication
through the other mother who was official escort for
both children, thus maintaining communication without actually collecting and fetching the child herself.

> Everyday I have a report. We have had terrible
> problems with Sam feeding. Everyday I like to
> know whether he has eaten any dinner..if he
> starts fussing around with his tea at night and
> I know he has had a big lunch, then I don't
> push it too hard, but if I know that he has not
> eaten anything..then I have to be sure that he
> gets a decent tea.

The mother who escorts converses daily with the
teacher in the classroom and in addition serves as a
volunteer dinner lady observing the feeding herself,
if not actually feeding Sam. Sam's mother, who
stated she did not want to be directly involved,
clearly wished to maintain access to information.

Other parents who wish to be actively involved
in doing school work at home find exchange of information essential.

> And then when he was learning to read and
> write, I heard what he was doing...I found it
> was very helpful to be able to reinforce.
> When he came home and was trying to do some-
> thing, at least I knew what he was trying to
> do.

Recalling joint work on toileting, one parent
argued how exchanging information on the child's
progress helped.

> The ideal - I liked to come in just two
> mornings a week - 'cause it was nice to just
> chat about what (they) had been doing in
> classroom, but the other useful thing was
> (their) notebook, that was very good
> actually...that was sufficient then to keep
> tabs on what she was doing and to be involved..

This parent found a combination of collecting and

fetching the child and a home-school notebook to be a satisfactory communication arrangement.

Another aspect of collecting and fetching the child that this parent values is the opportunity to build a relationship with the teacher, who initially refused to give the parent work to do with the child at home. The teacher gradually relented and the parent attributes this in part to the daily contact they had.

> ...that is a good chance of talking with the teacher and that's when she was asking about the grading and that's when you get most of the information....on a day-to-day basis. It is very useful to pick him up.

Information gathering of other kinds may take place through informal meetings at the classroom door. It may be the only opportunity parents have to meet the other children in the classroom and to gain some perspective on their own child's development and abilities. It gives parents a chance to assess their role in the care and education of their child and its impact on their lives.

> I mean we have only got to look around other handicapped children to realise that Sam is one of the worst handicapped...we have such a hectic time with him...I would go so far as to say Sam is about probably the most awkward, time-consuming child; that isn't just me saying it, I mean that is the teachers ...I mean I look at other kids and think "God, I could look after two of those as well as Sam and it probably wouldn't put me out one tiny bit."

It made her feel that the job she was doing was indeed difficult and that realistically she was not a 'fussing, nagging mother'. While this parent does not collect and fetch the child, close contact is maintained with the school. The teacher telephones if any problems arise and the parent said she can be at the school in seven minutes with ease. The school has made it clear that parents are welcome to visit, and that no appointment is necessary. As this parent viewed it, she could just 'breeze in' and was certain to be made to feel welcome.

Parents say that they acquire skills in an incidental manner, impossible to learn under more formal conditions. For example, one parent observed

a teacher dealing with a behaviour problem, a method
that she decided to try at home. Her description of
the incident reveals its impact.

> And she just got hold of Joan's hand, gently,
> firmly, she didn't grab her...and she said, "I
> think, Joan...it would be a good idea if you
> went up to your room and had a look at some of
> your books." And as she was saying it, she was
> walking her to the door...up she went and we
> never heard another muff out of her..."Yeah,"
> I thought, "yeah, I'm going to try that with
> Pauline when I get home."

This parent was extremely pleased to have achieved
the same result, successfully with her own child, a
major step forward from her point of view.

Parents reported learning about appropriate
educational material through contact with school,
enabling them to make wiser choices in gifts and
toys for their child.

> I know I got some smashing ideas from the
> classroom..with books and everything. And I
> went and bought these books and things like
> that, that I thought she would be able to do.

Finally, a parent noted how collecting and
fetching her child is the only opportunity she has
to meet other parents in the school. Through these
brief casual meetings, she has learned that they
have some mutual concerns and has been prompted to
think about what might be accomplished if parents
met regularly as a group. In her own words:

> It would be more useful to get to know the
> parents, 'cause I only know the parents...
> to speak to casually when I actually pick
> them up...I think we could give a concerted
> push if you like...in things like bringing
> your work home and also this business of
> transport 'cause I felt I was a lone voice
> until I realised that there were other
> mothers who felt the same way as I did.
> And also we would like to get to know the
> other parents of those people who go in the
> taxis. I find it useful talking to parents,
> other mothers in MENCAP say, just talking
> over difficulties at home and things like
> that..how they cope....swapping ideas and
> tips. I think that would be even more useful

where there are similar ages and the same classroom situation.

Thus, this informal short meeting of parents at the classroom door has stimulated thought about the worth of a more systematic approach to discussion with other parents.

CONCLUSION

While a transport service is often a valuable source of support, its use has implications broader than relieving stress, some of which parents perceive as disadvantageous to the child and family. Two areas that they claim to be primarily affected are integration and parent involvement. While collecting and fetching a child has hardly been viewed as an integral part of 'parent-involvement', as defined by professionals, it is clearly valued by parents because it permits regular unconstrained communication with the teacher and the school.

If present policy continues to move towards integration and parent involvement, then the practical implications for policy regarding a transport service are that it must be administered flexibly in response to individual families. Where children do use taxis, more thought needs to be given to finding means to ensure that regular informal access to the teacher and school is available to parents. Some successful alternatives have been mentioned but others could be explored.

REFERENCES

Paul, D. (1953) Interview techniques and field relationships. In A.L. Kroeber (ed.) Anthropology Today: An Encyclopedia Inventory. Chicago: University of Chicago Press
Spradley, P. (1979) The Ethnographic Interview. New York: Holt, Rinehart and Winston

DISCUSSION

Papers eight and nine were discussed together. Barbara Smith stressed that professionals bear the primary responsibility for the creation of good parent-professional relations. Her reasons included the fact that professionals are more likely to be in touch with recent changes in the techniques and attitudes of service-providers than parents, particularly those of older mentally handicapped children, and therefore that it is the responsibility of professionals to discuss these with parents. Many parents do not know, for example, that they have a legal right to be present when their child is examined by a doctor or a psychologist. She also felt that, as well as talking with parents about their practical and emotional needs, discussing 'professional' issues will contribute to the development of a trusting relationship. However, it is important to be careful about the language used in talking with parents and writing reports on the child, so that parents feel confident and fully understand. She urged that much greater attention should be paid to these aspects of co-operation with parents in the training of teachers.

Christoph Hublow from Germany, who is also a teacher, said that both the preceding papers had asked the right question: "Why should parents *not* be involved?" He wanted more practical discussion and guidelines on how exactly to best involve parents in assessments and case-conferences, and help parents understand the scientific background of special education. It became clear in discussion that schools vary widely in how parents and teachers collaborate in practice. There were also national differences in expectations about the proper content of education (see Chapter 13). There is an enormous gulf to bridge if parents think education is about reading, writing and arithmetic, while teachers think in terms of helping the child to acquire practical skills and ways of communicating with others; or the other way round. Considerable obstacles to partnership can arise from the preconceptions parents and teachers have about each other's roles.

Mariet van Hattum commented that in Holland home-school notebooks are commonly used in describing to parents what the child has done in school during the day. But the drawbacks of such a system include its formality, and the families' lack of contact with each other. She herself experienced the 'special little bus' which took her daughter to school as a source of humiliation (ie. arising from her own feelings) rather than of discrimination (arising from the world outside), and other parents had told her they had similar difficult feelings. Special transport seems to emphasise the inevitability of the handicap. She suggested that there was probably no real solution to the problem, as it was having a handicapped child which hurt parents, rather than any one particular aspect of the whole.

Many participants considered that relationships between parents and teachers would be greatly improved in future with the advent of early intervention. In some parts of Britain, the main regular contact which families with a mentally handicapped baby experience is with some kind of peripatetic teacher, for example, in the Portage Projects. Apart from the benefits to the child's development, this collaboration also helps parents to get used and to expect to work with professionals.

Chapter 10

SCHOOL-BASED PARENT INVOLVEMENT: A PSYCHOLOGIST'S VIEW

Jill Gardner

It has often been argued that the education of handicapped children is a highly skilled task which should only be carried out by specially trained staff. While I would agree that there are many good reasons why special school staff should be highly trained, I do not feel that this need in any way exclude parents from the educational process, since there are many ways in which the active inclusion of parents can greatly enhance the educational opportunities of children with special needs.

Of the total time available for teaching the handicapped child during his or her lifetime, a relatively short period of time will be spent in school. This, coupled with the need to ensure generalisation of skills learned in school to other settings, provides a strong motive for schools to involve parents as active participants in the learning process. A policy of parental involvement should also ensure that families become more aware of their children's capabilities, and in taking a positive approach towards their children, will be less likely to find themselves coping alone with possibly increasingly disruptive behaviour problems.

School-based parental involvement also encourages parents to help each other, eg. by forming self-help groups, thus reducing the likelihood of the social isolation of families with a handicapped child. These self-supporting groups can also be used by other professionals as a vehicle for more general discussion with parents who experience common worries and problems concerned with the medical aspects of handicap, the services available to them in the community and so on. Above all, parent involvement can ensure that teachers and parents work together on an equal footing for the benefit of the children, thus breaking down long-established

barriers between those who are trained to teach
handicapped children and those who live with them.

Awareness of the importance of parental involvement in teaching their children has led to the
development of a variety of well-documentated projects which differ widely in purpose and organisation. Reviews of these projects can be found elsewhere, so I shall now consider just a few examples,
before discussing the ways in which the skills of
teachers and the school curriculum can be used in
parental involvement.

INDIVIDUAL THERAPIST/FAMILY INVOLVEMENT

Many individual studies of 'parents as therapists'
have been documented which illustrate the effectiveness of parent training by another professional in
the management of problem behaviours or in the training of new skills (e.g. Sandow and Clarke, 1978).
Traditionally, this model of parental involvement is
not school-based, but involves the therapist (often a
psychologist) in setting up a teaching or management
programme which is put into action between therapy
sessions by the parents. Using this individual
model to teach new skills, staff involved in the
Portage Projects (Shearer and Shearer, 1972) have
been able to demonstrate a rapid increase in the
acquisition of new skills in pre-school handicapped
children who were taught at home by their parents,
with assistance and regular visits from specially
trained home teachers.

The model of individual parent/therapist involvement has two main advantages but several disadvantages. The advantages are that the parent is
actively included in the training of the child
and that the model has a built-in evaluation system
in that the success or failure of intervention is
directly measured in terms of the child's performance. The disadvantages of this approach are that
it is extremely costly in terms of therapist time;
it lacks planned involvement of other family members,
which is potentially undermining both to the 'main
parent' and to the others; there is potential dependency on the therapist in weekly visiting, with the
danger of reducing parent confidence; the parents
are not given an opportunity to form self-supporting
groups; and there is no planned link between programmes used for the child in school and at home.

It is worth noting here that the Portage Project
in particular was designed to meet the needs of
families with pre-school handicapped children who had

no access to pre-school facilities and who were
living in a large geographical area, so that there
was no opportunity for the disadvantages inherent in
this model to be overcome.

GROUP THERAPIST/FAMILY INVOLVEMENT

Many of the disadvantages of individual parent
support can be overcome where parents are brought
together in groups to discuss their special children's problems and/or to be given practical advice
by a therapist. This group parental involvement
model has been used in a variety of settings, for
example, as part of a research facility (Cunningham
and Jeffree, 1971); as an evening course at an Adult
Education Centre (Cummings, 1975); and as part of a
school-based facility (Bevington, Gardner and Cocks,
1981). In this wide variety of settings, parents
can not only receive guidance in the management of
their children in a way which is an efficient use of
therapist time, but they can also form self-supporting social groups. Though these groups are advantageous in many ways, it becomes much more difficult
to evaluate their effectiveness. The advantages of
forming a self-help group would be difficult to
measure, and since the children are not directly involved in the group, methods need to be found to
measure the effect of therapist/parent interaction
in terms of changes in child behaviour.
    These difficulties of evaluation may in part
explain the paucity of data collected during parent
involvement projects. Burden (1978) aimed to measure changes in maternal attitudes during such intervention, and in several studies reports are given of
parents' subjective views of the helpfulness of parent workshop course (eg. Cummings, 1975). Rarely
does there seem to be any attempt to evaluate
changes in parents' knowledge or use of teaching
techniques, except by the use of anecdotal evidence.

EVALUATION OF LOCAL PARENT WORKSHOPS

During our involvement with local authority schools
for the severely mentally handicapped (ESNS), we
have developed a number of parent workshops which
were jointly planned by psychologists and teachers,
and held in schools. Since we were at that time new
to this field of work ourselves, we felt that it
would be very important to find out how well we were
communicating our ideas and skills to parents, so
that we could modify our course for the future.

Evaluation should form an integral part of course planning, rather than an 'optional extra' tacked on to the last session. In other words, before one can find out what effects have been produced, it is vital to list the effects which are being sought, and to plan teaching strategies accordingly. Since we had, in teaching children, evaluated the effectiveness of our teaching in terms of specific skills learned by them, we felt that we should follow the same procedure when teaching parents.

Our original study is documented in detail elsewhere (Bevington, et al., 1978). In summary, we started by writing general aims for our workshop, which were derived from specific needs outlined to us by parents in an initial interview. From these general aims, we listed a number of targets which we felt it would be important for parents to master in order for their general needs to be met. Originally these specific targets were written in terms of the parents' ability to use teaching techniques in simulated teaching situations and their ability to answer correctly questions designed to test their theoretical knowledge of the areas covered. Less emphasis was placed upon their attempts to teach new skills to their children at home. We later realised that this was a mistake.

Having devised specific targets, we were then in a position to plan our teaching methods: that is, we could decide how many sessions to run, how to present the material and so on. We were also able to collect specific information from parents so that we could find out to what extent they had in fact learned the skills which we had set out to teach.

The information gained was encouraging, since many of the parents had in fact mastered the pre-set targets. We were also encouraged by parents' regular attendance and their positive comments. At the end of the course, we again visited the families at home to try to find out what effect, if any, the course had had on their attempts to teach their children at home. It became very clear that we had not developed any reliable means of gathering evidence of behaviour change on the part of the parents, and that a change in 'verbal behaviour' (i.e. what parents' can say, write, etc) as a result of the course was no guarantee whatever of parental behaviour change in the home.

EFFECTS ON PARENTS' SKILLS

Our subsequent projects therefore have had a different emphasis. We have recently been much more concerned with planning, teaching, and evaluating effective means of teaching parents practical skills, and have de-emphasised the need for verbalisation of theoretical information.

In our most recent study, parents were invited to join the workshop and were told specifically that the group was designed to assist them in teaching skills to their children. The parents who volunteered were visited at home and asked to demonstrate for us a short teaching session with their child. During this initial observation we were able to record, for example :

- the task chosen by the parent (eg. toilet training, colour discrimination, self-help skills);
- the way in which instructions were given by the parent;
- the ways in which the parent reacted when the child succeeded at the task;
- the ways in which parents tried to give children extra help if the task was proving too difficult; and so on.

All of these observations were measured against the skills which we planned to teach the parents by the end of the workshop. Thus, we now had some objective data on parents' teaching skills.

From these observations we were able to construct a list of targets for the parents; in other words, we were able to specify those skills which we were planning to teach parents during the course of the sessions. From these targets we were then able to plan our teaching methods as before. Since we were emphasising parents' abilities to use the teaching techniques in practice with their children, we tried to ensure that sufficient time was given for parents to learn these new practical skills, by showing videotaped demonstrations, organising discussions and group practical sessions.

Half of the families who attended the workshops were also visited at home in between sessions so that parents could practise their teaching skills at home with supervision from ourselves. The skill areas covered during the sessions included :

- gaining the child's attention and co-operation;

- ensuring that the child was given consistent and simple task instructions;
- techniques to be used when the child failed on the task, e.g. the use of prompts;
- the assessment and use of rewards;
- training of the child to imitate;
- planning programmes by breaking tasks down into simple steps;
- recording progress.

It was felt that these skills were essential for parents to have mastered if they were to be successful in teaching their children at home.

At the end of the course, parents were again asked to complete questionnaires, which gave us information both on their views about the usefulness of the course, and some indication of their ability to verbalise their knowledge of the teaching techniques we had covered. Knowing now that this was important but insufficient information, we again visited families at home and made observations on a single teaching session which the parents conducted with their own children.

In summary, our results once again indicated significant and positive change in parents' verbal behaviour (i.e. what they could say, write, etc, about the teaching techniques). However, we also found a marked discrepancy between the actual teaching abilities of those parents who had been given guided practice sessions at home and those who had only attended the course without any extra support. Those parents who had been given an opportunity to practise their skills with constructive feedback from ourselves were much more able to conduct a teaching session which more nearly resembled the list of skills involved which we had originally devised. These results are not very surprising in retrospect, but they do illustrate once again the importance both of careful planning and of evaluation of expected post-course outcomes.

Despite the fact that we felt that we had started to make some progress in terms of our increased efficiency as parent trainers, we were confronted with another problem. While many parents could, under optimum conditions, exhibit proficient teaching skills, we also discovered that parents were not teaching their children either often enough or for long enough, and were finding it difficult to keep careful records. In other words, parents now *had* improved teaching skills, but were not *utilising* them to greatest effect.

What reasons could we find for this? Obviously, motivation to help their children was not in doubt, since they had volunteered for the course, had attended regularly, and were still regular visitors to formal and informal gatherings held at school. The problem seemed to stem not from a lack of enthusiasm but from a lack of specific direction. Although parents now had teaching skills, they were often unsure which task to choose, and after the course ended there was no planned follow-up to give further guidance or suggest teaching areas to them.

USING THE SCHOOL CURRICULUM

The problems which parents experience in choosing appropriate tasks and in keeping careful records of their children's progress can be overcome if the school has developed a structured curriculum. In using a behavioural curriculum model, teachers in the school will have selected appropriate teaching targets for each child. They will have done this by first assessing each child's skill levels, using the curriculum as an assessment procedure. By breaking down each target skill into a step by step programme, they will then be able to select an appropriate teaching step. By using record forms, they will have an accurate record of the child's progress.

Because this detailed information is already available in school, there is no need for parents either to choose a teaching target in an arbitrary fashion or for them to be given a separate observation schedule (such as a developmental checklist) to help them in their teaching. Instead, teachers will be able to tell the parents exactly what the child has learned in school and precisely which targets are currently being taught. In this way parents can either assist school staff by sharing the teaching of the weekly target or targets, or by assisting the generalisation process through teaching targets already learned in school, under the different conditions of home, or in other settings.

There may still be concern in teachers' minds that parents may try to teach skills by using different instructions or different materials to those used in school. Using a behavioural curriculum, these problems can be avoided: firstly by ensuring that the teaching skills taught to parents in the group match up as far as possible with those used by teachers in school; secondly, targets and steps in the school curriculum are very clearly specified, with the instructions to be given and materials to be used written into the programme. This not only means that different teachers are more likely to teach these skills in the same way, but it also assists parents, and gives them very precise quidelines.

Record-keeping by parents is also facilitated since it is an integral part of the programme, and separate different record forms do not need to be produced for use by parents: rather it would be preferable if they were given duplicates of the class teachers' record forms for their use at home.

Perhaps the greatest advantage of using the school curriculum in this way is the effect that this has on parent motivation. Instead of home and school working separately with each child, parents and teachers can more easily work together to achieve the same result. The fact that parents are thus seen working alongside the teacher has enormous benefits for all concerned. The parent knows that after a period of teaching the child at home, there will be detailed information to bring back to school in the form of data on the record form. Parents and teachers can then enjoy a much more useful discussion on the child's learning, problems arising from the use of the programme, and so on. When a target is achieved, parents will know that they will again be involved in working with the teacher on the selection of the next appropriate teaching target. Thus, the emphasis of parent involvement groups can shift away from a series of lectures or discussions, towards a permanent collaboration, which should be maintained until the child leaves school.

In terms of practical arrangements, there are a variety of ways in which this ideal situation could be achieved. This will depend upon the number of families interested in working in this way, and the availability of staff either during or after school time. One possible means of organising such a venture might be to run a short series of weekly workshops after school to cover aspects relating to parents' acquisition of teaching skills. Thereafter meetings could be held less often - say once a month - at which parents could discuss progress, and be given new targets to work on where appropriate.

CONCLUSION

This chapter discusses the contribution which parents can make to the education of their children and suggests some ways in which schools might involve parents in the teaching process. Parental involvement requires careful planning if it is to be successful. A school which uses a behavioural model for curriculum planning has readily available a number of resources which can be utilised by parents to the greater advantage of the children. This also ensures that a more meaningful evaluation of parental involvement can be carried out, since measures of changes in child behaviour are being collected continuously both at home and at school.

REFERENCES

Bevington, P., Gardner, J.M. and Cocks, R.P. (1978) An approach to the planning and evaluation of a parental involvement course. Child: Care, Health and Development, 4, 217-227

Burden, R.L. (1978) An approach to the evaluation of early intervention projects with mothers of severely handicapped children: the attitude dimension. Child: Care, Health and Development, 4, 171-181

Cocks, R.P. and Gardner, J.M. (1978) Parent workshops. Apex, 6 (2), 18-19

Cummings, P. (1975) You and your handicapped child. Unpublished paper, School Psychological Service, Birmingham.

Cunningham, C.C. and Jeffree, D.M. (1971) Working with Parents: Developing a Workshop Course for Parents of Young Mentally Handicapped Children. Manchester: National Society for Mentally Handicapped Children

Sandow, S. and Clarke, A.D.B. (1978) Home intervention with parents of severely subnormal, pre-school children: an interim report. Child: Care, Health and Development, 4, 29-39

Shearer, M.S. and Shearer, D.E. (1972) The Portage Project - a model for early childhood education. Exceptional Children, 39, 201-207

DISCUSSION

As a preliminary to discussion, Jill Gardner gave a description of two series of workshops in which she had been involved, of a very different kind from those described in her paper. One was for a group of Asian mothers, initiated by the school because the contact with this group was felt to be insufficient. The families were invited for a series of six visits to the school. They were shown the kind of tasks that their children were doing in school

174

and were involved in helping their children at meal-time and in play sessions. A member of staff of the local authority Social Services Department also talked to the parents about their rights and where to go for help and information locally. The other workshop was for parents of school-leavers and aimed at providing information and discussion about subsequent provision such as Adult Training Centres and hostels.

Christopher Hublow questioned whether teaching was a task which parents should take on, and stressed the need to remain *parents* who try to provide at home a loving, natural family setting for all their children, and by doing so balance the handicapped child's systematic training at school. He suggested that teaching might create distance and emotional disturbance between parent and child. He also questioned the behavioural curriculum model, suggesting it was too narrow a framework for all of education. For example, how could parents be helped to find interesting and challenging leisure events and social activities for their children?

Jill Gardner replied to the concern about emotional distance being created between parent and child by emphasising that parents had been given very pessimistic prognoses in the past, with concentration on what the child could not do. Therefore, an accent on the positive, and on what parents *can* do to help, fosters confidence in the parents and brings them closer to the child as they experience success in teaching.

Cliff Cunningham also pointed out that learning about teaching skills would not only have the aim of helping parents with their child, but would also tend to increase their understanding of the work of teachers, thus making a dialogue easier.

SECTION FIVE: ADOLESCENCE AND ADULTHOOD

Chapter 11

WORKING WITH PARENTS OF ADOLESCENTS: THE WORK OF THE PATH PROJECT

Dorothy Jeffree and Sally Cheseldine

The approach to parental involvement discussed in this chapter arises out of a four year research project, Parents and Their Handicapped Teenagers, concerned particularly with the leisure time activities of these young people. It explores their knowledge of and participation in various pastimes, their patterns of friendship and levels of socialization, as well as the concerns of their parents.

WHY PARENTS?

At an age when mentally handicapped teenagers are being helped to become increasingly independent, why do we work with parents?

1. Parents or parent substitutes have the greatest individual effect on any child's development.

2. The time any child or young person spends at home is greater than the time spent at school.

3. At a time of transition on leaving school, when teenagers are faced with an environmental change, a change from familiar personnel, a break from friends and a new regime, parents form the only stable link.

4. Parents remain the decision makers and a young person's future will largely depend upon the parents' continued ability to cope, e.g. whether or not they ask for residential care for the young person.

5. Parents of today's adolescents have received very little help in the past but may need special advice and assistance at this critical time.

WHY ADOLESCENTS?

Families may be faced with critical decisions throughout their child's life. Why have we chosen to concentrate on the period of adolescence?

1. Leaving school is a critical period for any adolescent who has to cope with physical, mental, emotional and environmental change. Without help, mentally handicapped young people may be ill-equipped or unready to make this step and their lives may become more restricted, rather than less restricted as in the case of a non-handicapped teenager.

2. Although there is increasing help for pre-school and school age mentally handicapped children, what about those who were born too soon to benefit from these changes? Changes are only just beginning to take place in provision for adolescents and adults. It is never too late to learn and mentally handicapped individuals, deprived of early stimulation and training, have been able to benefit from structured programmes later in life (Clarke and Clarke, 1976).

3. At adolescence many mentally handicapped teenagers are only just reaching the developmental level of normal children starting school (Marshall, 1967). At a time when they could benefit from educational, social and recreational programmes they may be least likely to have the opportunity to do so.

WHY LEISURE?

At a time when human worth is usually equated with socio-economic status at work, why do we choose to concentrate on leisure?

1. "The normalizing potential of recreation is yet to be realized ... unfortunately mentally retarded adults who are proficient at their jobs may fail to adjust to community life because they are not aware of recreational resources available to them, or have not learnt how to use them" (Luckey and Shapiro, 1974).

2. All school leavers now have more time on

their hands, often being unable to get work. This has nearly always been the case for mentally handicapped people.

3. Many parents of the handicapped speak of their isolation within the community. This may be even greater for handicapped people themselves. Properly programmed leisure activities have great potential for integration.

4. The importance of play in the social, emotional and intellectual development of children is not in doubt. For mentally handicapped people, this period of childhood play may need to be extended and accepted until they are ready to partake in the leisure time activities of their normal peers

A SURVEY OF SCHOOL LEAVERS

Although the abilities of children leaving Junior Training Centres in the 1960's were charted by Marshall (1967), there is scant information on the abilities of children currently leaving ESNS schools and even less on their home situation. For this reason a survey of all the known ESNS school leavers in the Greater Manchester Area (214), 87 per cent of total, was carried out by the PATH Project (see Cheseldine and Jeffree (1982) for a full report).

The homes were visited and the informants were the parents supplemented by information from the young people themselves. A checklist of self-help skills — *Pathways to Independence* (Jeffree and Cheseldine, 1982) - was prepared and each teenager's present status in ten areas of self-help was charted. In addition a semi-structured interview was carried out and the parents reported on their son or daughter's leisure time activities and friendship pattern, as well as being given an opportunity to identify problems and difficulties and to make suggestions. Some of the findings will be reported in the context of the main discussion.

The Home
The majority of ESNS children live at home, only 9.5 per cent of the 214 teenagers being in residential care. However, when children leave school and become adults, the parents themselves are also growing older and their continued ability to cope becomes problematic. When their children leave school, parents become increasingly concerned with

what is going to happen when they die. Many feel
that it would be unfair to pass on the burden of
responsibility to siblings who have their own lives
to lead.

In our survey 83 per cent of the fathers were
over 40 and seven per cent over 60 (Cheseldine and
Jeffree, 1981b). We note that the years between 16
and 20 are the peak period for admission to mental
handicap hospitals (National Development Group,
1978).

Planning for the Future

Individually and communally it is important not to
be put off doing anything about the future until a
crisis occurs but to plan in good time. Nationally,
as the National Development Group (1978) suggest, we
need to develop community services to prevent inappropriate hospital admission. Individually there
is also much that can be done to prepare young
people to live more independently (Mittler,
Cheseldine and McConachie, 1981). Information
gleaned from the parents in our survey has highlighted some important areas of concern where
ideally action should be taken before the young
people leave school.

Pathways to Independence

A minority of mentally handicapped adults do become
sufficiently independent of their families to be
able to lead relatively autonomous lives in the
community. If we mapped out the pathways that lead
to this degree of independence, their number could
perhaps be greatly increased. We should also consider the obstacles that lie in the way of independence and how far along the road each individual
has already come.

Hannam (1980) suggests that sometimes the mentally handicapped are less dependent when away from
their homes and can do things which parents thought
were quite beyond them. In this context, we need to
provide opportunities for them to practise the
skills they already possess as well as helping them
to develop new skills in priority areas.

Our survey suggests that most parents have done
a very good job in ensuring that their son/daughters
are reasonably independent within the home environment. Their achievement must not be underestimated, for it is often quicker to do things for
others than to teach them to help themselves. Most
of the young people in our survey needed no assistance in eating and drinking (77 per cent) or toilet-

182

ing (58 per cent). They also helped with the household chores and over 50 per cent could set and clear the table, about a third were able to wash and dry dishes on their own and put them away and 46 per cent could make their own beds.

Having started on the path towards independence, we need to consider some of the priority areas in which extra help may be needed. For instance, for an independent existence a young person needs to be able to prepare a simple meal. But although most of the young people in our survey were able to prepare a cold drink (77 per cent) and many a hot drink (51 per cent), only three per cent could prepare a simple meal on their own.

We found that most of the young people went shopping 'en famille', though a few were sent on errands to nearby local shops. However, very few went further afield on their own and only two per cent were reported as able to use public transport independently, even on a familiar route. One of the difficulties seemed to be in the handling of money – and here there seemed to be a lack of opportunity as well as of skill. We found that many of the young people were never given pocket money of their own to handle and that money was handed over to them only for specific purchases. Only six per cent of the young people could combine coins and notes to a specific value.

Many schools are well aware of these priority areas and have instituted training programmes to ensure that initial disabilities do not become lasting handicaps. However, unless these skills are also practised at home, their work may be in vain. How this might be achieved will be discussed later.

Integration
The importance of peer group friendships can hardly be overemphasized, for even amongst the handicapped themselves, two friends will have complementary skills and disabilities and can often accomplish far more than either could achieve on their own.

Many parents were concerned about their child's isolation from the local community of peers. They reported that when the children were younger they were accepted by the other small children and played with them amicably, but as they grew older the gap widened and the other local children 'didn't want to know'. The situation was exacerbated by the handicapped teenager's increasing self-consciousness. The young people who were the most fully accepted were often those who had attended normal schools and

retained their school friends or who lived in more
impoverished inner city areas.

In this .context we found that, although the
majority of young people had one or more specific
friends at school and their parents often knew of
them, yet only a quarter ever visited their school
friends out of school hours. In some cases, the
parents had overlooked the importance of such
friendships but the geographical distances involved
made visiting impracticable and lack of independent
mobility on the teenagers' part made this even more
difficult. The parents themselves contributed an
interesting point. They pointed out that they did
not know the parents of their handicapped children's
school friends very well. It was different with
their normal children; contact with other parents
was made early on at the nursery or infant school
gate and family visits followed naturally.

The Forgotten Hours
We know that a mentally handicapped young person
spends more hours at home than anywhere else, in
spite of the increase in special holidays, expeditions and clubs which give their parents a welcome
relief. The parents themselves are very well aware
of these 'forgotten hours' of weekends, long
holidays and evenings. The way in which these hours
are filled, in frustration or lethargy or constructively, may have a direct bearing on the families'
continued ability to cope. However, little information has been available as to how they were spent.
Such thoughts prompted us to include in our survey
information from the parents on the teenagers'
leisure time pursuits when at home (Cheseldine and
Jeffree, 1981).

Nash (1953) has suggested a hierarchy of
leisure pursuits. The lowest level of this hierarchy is spectator activities, through activities
with greater involvement and those with increased
socialization, to highly creative activities. A
handicapped person may remain at the lowest level of
this hierarchy without specific intervention. As
Bates and Renzaglia (1979) remarked, "The constructive use of leisure time depends to a great extent
upon the skills and interests an individual has
acquired and these skills and interests develop as
the result of planned, systematic experience with
specific activities". Katz and Yekutiel (1974) add,
"Handicapped individuals often spend long periods of
time engaged in passive activities like watching
television because they have not acquired the skills

184

for engaging in a greater diversity of leisure time activities". Although the situation had been reported in America, very little was known about mentally handicapped teenagers' use of leisure in England and no systematic attempt had been made to help teenagers to acquire the skills necessary for a greater diversity of leisure time occupation.

The Handicapped Teenagers' Use of Leisure Time
The parents or guardians listed their son or daughter's leisure time occupations in a semi-structured interview. The four most frequently mentioned occupations were listening to tapes of records (89 per cent), watching TV (87 per cent) or going shopping (70 per cent). The shopping mainly consisted of expeditions with other members of the family. A hobby such as painting or drawing was mentioned by 31 per cent and knitting or sewing by 12 per cent. It can be seen that the most frequently mentioned activities are comparatively passive and do not require much personal involvement or interaction with other people.

Did these activities arise from choice or because without the necessary skills or friends there were few alternatives available? A partial answer to this question could be gained by planning systematic programmes to train a variety of alternative leisure time activities and seeing how the young people chose to occupy themselves after they had acquired these skills. In order to put this to the test, we carried out several pilot studies in which we observed the young people in free choice situations and recorded what they did. We then trained them individually on a programmed series of table games of chance and observed their behaviour when these games also were available. The observation sessions were carried out both at school and at home. Once they had acquired the skills to engage in new activities, there was a significant difference in the pupils' behaviour. In a free choice situation both at school and at home, there was a decrease in solitary activities and an increase in skilled interactive pursuits. At home, before the introduction of the games, 56 per cent of the reported activities were solitary but after the introduction of the games this dropped to 39 per cent. Once the skills had been acquired, the handicapped teenagers were able to play with others on equal terms.

Home and School Links

"The school is obviously the greatest help the parents receive. What is less satisfactory than the progress the school has achieved with the child, continues to be the quality of communication with the school." (Hannam, 1980)

Our experience also suggests that the quality of communication between home and school is less than satisfactory. This was our conclusion in spite of the fact that parents were loyal and appreciative of what the schools were doing and most schools had some form of Parent Teacher Association. However only a minority of parents attend the meetings. Possible reasons for this non-attendance will obviously vary from school to school; one of the most obvious is the distance of home from school and transport difficulties. Pupils are transported to school by taxis or special buses but parents find it difficult to make their own way to school, especially when both are working. There is no easy solution to this problem, though one school has used the school minibus to pick up parents for evening meetings which then have very high rates of attendance. More important still, to what extent do these meetings meet the parents' real needs? Very few parents suggested that they did not. A few mentioned a somewhat excessive emphasis on fund raising.

We were particularly concerned about how little some of the parents seemed to know of what went on in school, and conversely, how little the teachers knew of what went on at home, though home and school activities should have been complementary. For example, one mother did not allow her son near the cooker in the kitchen and said he could not make hot drinks or toast and then added the comment, "I think he does it at school, but I am not sure". As Hannam (1980) remarked, "Surely the school and parents must aim at approaching the problem of education jointly rather than separately". Careful planning and preparation will be needed in order for this to come about. One way in which this has been done successfully in this country is through parent workshops (Cunningham and Jeffree, 1971).

WORKSHOPS

Some schools have started workshops for parents of their top classes. In these workshops, parents and teachers work together as equals. Other professionals such as speech therapists, physiotherapists and psychologists are invited for some of the sessions. In preparation for the workshop, both parents and teachers complete the Pathways to Independence checklist independently for each pupil (Jeffree and Cheseldine, 1982). The first session is given over to the discussion of any discrepancies which appear in the two versions of the checklist and the reasons for these differences, e.g. behaviour at school and at home is often different, one place provides opportunities that the other does not, parents have knowledge of early development which the teachers have not, misunderstandings may arise in the interpretation of some items, both parties may have a tendency to over- or under-estimate the pupils. Frank discussion of these differences prepares the way for the planning and implementation of joint programmes.

We also found that many parents were very vague about provision for school leavers, although their children were due to leave school shortly. Staff from Adult Training Centres, and Colleges of Further Education can be invited to the workshop sessions to fill this gap and alleviate some parental anxiety.

Hannam (1980) has said, "Parents have to fight for their rights - the initiative comes from them". He also suggests that working class families are often less successful in getting help than middle class families. The workshop experience gives these parents increased self-confidence and a realisation that they have an important contribution to make.

Perhaps one of the biggest contributions the workshops have to make is providing a venue in which parents can get to know one another better. The outcome of one workshop was the sharing of leisure time activities. One parent who was very well provided with leisure time facilities threw these open to her daughter's friends and to other normal teenagers, which was a start towards further integration.

QUESTIONS FOR THE FUTURE

In this chapter we have posed questions for the future on the issues of parent-professional collaboration and on recreation and leisure for the mentally handicapped school leaver. In conclusion we will select a few of the leading questions which call for immediate attention.

1. *Are we satisfied with the present level of parent/ professional involvement and, if not, what can be done to improve matters?*

Parents of mentally handicapped children are only too ready to shoulder responsibility for their child; the majority of these children live at home, where they spend more time than anywhere else and are included in most family activities and outings and holidays. This means that parents continually live with their anxieties about the future which they are usually powerless to alleviate.

Professionals could do much to reduce these anxieties. There is an obvious need for an extension of educational, recreational and residential provision, and also, with help, many more young people could become less of a burden to their families, more independent and integrated into the community. However, unilateral training in independent living skills which are never practised at home is unlikely to be effective. Parents and professionals need to work together to plan and implement programmes.

Professionals may justifiably answer that opportunities already exist for discussions with parents but they are not taken up by the majority of parents. This dilemma raises a number of important issues:

. is the right kind of help being offered?
. have parents been consulted on the time and place of meeting?
. is transport available?
. is provision made for the rest of the family?
. are parents given prior information on what is being offered?
. are parents treated as fellow professionals?

Where efforts have been made to answer these questions parent participation has increased.

2. *Should we be giving greater consideration to ways of providing satisfying alternatives to paid employment, that is "significant living without work"* (Warnock, 1978)? We live in a society which still adheres to the work ethic but is developing in such a way as to reduce employment possibilities, especially for the mentally handicapped. The functions which paid employment fulfils have been summarised by Tizard and Anderson (1978) as giving the individual a sense of identity, a feeling of contributing to society, financial independence, an opportunity for social contacts and a structure to the day. They go on to suggest alternative ways in which these functions can be fulfilled for the physically and mentally handicapped school leaver who is unable to gain paid

188

employment. In this chapter we have suggested ways in which leisure time activities can fulfil some of these functions, especially in giving the individual opportunities for social contacts, a structure to the day and a feeling of personal identity through the exercise of choice.

There are signs that recreation and leisure are beginning to be taken seriously. Recently an O.E.C.D conference was given over to the topic of "The education and social integration of handicapped children through recreational activities" and follow-up seminars are taking place in the participating countries. Although much of the emphasis of this conference was on organised outdoor activities for the physically disabled (horse riding, swimming etc.) one of the key issues which arose from the conference was the need for *early* induction into the use of leisure (Neale, 1982). This is particularly important when we are considering mentally handicapped people.

How can we ensure that every individual is given a start, how ever low down on the hierarchy of leisure activities? What is the first step towards socialisation through recreation, which can eventually lead to integration into the community and use of community facilities? As most of leisure time is spent at home, how can we involve the family in taking that first step? Finally, to what extent is systematic teaching being used to facilitate recreational skills in schools?

REFERENCES

Bates, P. & Renzaglia, A. (1979) Community based recreation programs. In P. Wehman (ed.) Recreation Programming for Developmentally Disabled Persons. Baltimore: University Park Press

Cheseldine, S.E. & Jeffree, D.M. (1981) Mentally handicapped adolescents: their use of leisure. Journal of Mental Deficiency Research, 25, 49-59

Cheseldine, S.E. & Jeffree, D.M. (1982) Mentally handicapped adolescents: a survey of abilities. Special Education: Forward Trends (research supplement), 9, 19-23

Clarke, A.M. & Clark, A.D.B. (1976) Early Experience: Myth and Evidence. London: Open Books

Cunningham, C.C. & Jeffree, D.M. (1971) Working with Parents: Developing a Workshop Course for

Parents of Young Mentally Handicapped Children.
   Manchester: National Society for Mentally
   Handicapped Children (North-West Region).
   (5th edition, 1979)
Hannam, C. (1980) Parents and Mentally Handicapped
   Children, 2nd edition. Harmondsworth: Penguin
Jeffree, D.M. & Cheseldine, S.E. (1982) Pathways to
   Independence: a Checklist of Self-Help Activi-
   ties. London: Hodder & Stoughton
Katz, S. & Yekutiel, E. (1974) Leisure time problems
   of mentally retarded graduates of training pro-
   grammes. Mental Retardation, 12, 54-57
Luckey, R.E. & Shapiro, I.G. (1974) Recreation: an
   essential aspect of habilitative programming.
   Mental Retardation, 12, 33-45
Marshall, A. (1967) The Abilities and Attainments of
   Children Leaving Junior Training Centres.
   London: National Association for Mental Health
Mittler, P., Cheseldine, S. and McConachie, H.
   (1981) Roles and Needs of Parents of Handi-
   capped Adolescents. Paris: Organisation for
   Economic Cooperation and Development (CERI)
National Development Group (1977) Helping Mentally
   Handicapped School Leavers. London: DHSS
National Development Group (1978) Helping Mentally
   Handicapped People in Hospital. London: DHSS
Nash, J.B. (1953) Philosophy of Recreation and
   Leisure. Dubuque, Iowa: William C. Brown
Neale, M.D. (1982) An overview and summary of pro-
   ceedings. In The Education and Social Inte-
   gration of Handicapped Children through Recre-
   ational Activities, Report of an International
   Seminar. Paris: Organisation for Economic Co-
   operation and Development
Tizard, J. and Anderson, E. (1978) The Education of
   the Handicapped Adolescent: an Interim Report
   of the First Phase of the Project. Paris:
   Organisation for Economic Cooperation and
   Development
Warnock, H.M. (1978) Special Educational Needs.
   Report of the Committee of Enquiry into the
   Education of Handicapped Children and Young
   People. Cmnd. 7212. London: HMSO

DISCUSSION

In opening the discussion of their paper, Dorothy
Jeffree and Sally Cheseldine mentioned that all the
parents they had met in the course of their
research had been very polite and helpful and
willing to answer their questions. They understood

that the investigation might further the improvement
of services for mentally handicapped young people.
However, many voiced feelings of disappointment that
this attention from professionals came too late.

The parents of this generation did not have the
chance to benefit from the kind of services which
currently offer help as early as possible. They did
not have the chance to get used to working with professionals. Possibly as a result of this, many did
not make use of opportunities that were available to
them; for example, few of the parents in the survey
ever attended meetings of the Parent Teacher Association of their child's school.

Even though the actual number of severely ment-
all handicapped school-leavers is small (estimated
at 4 or 5 per 100,000 total population per year)
preparation and planning for this critical period
are very unsatisfactory. We still do not often
arrange multidisciplinary assessments and plans for
the teenagers' future after leaving school. In
order to meet their needs better, families must have
information about the options which are open, perhaps through 'Careers Conventions' and 'Leisure Conventions', bringing together teachers, staff of
adult services and of colleges of further education,
social workers, parents and the mentally handicapped
adolescents themselves.

Dorothy Jeffree emphasised the importance for
the good practice of professionals of learning from
collaboration with parents. Yet this must be temp-
ered with common sense: 'making relationships with
parents' obviously takes time because making
relationships with people takes time. Professionals
must also learn to judge when they are adding unduly
to the pressures on parents, by raising expectations
of the parental role.

Professionals will sometimes be faced with the
problem of conveying to parents their assessment
that the adolescent is being kept more dependent
than necessary by the parents' handling. Parents
may not feel able to provide opportunities for the
young person to practice skills of independence and
self-reliance. Such pressures may result in residential placement for the young person, because the
family feels they cannot cope any longer, rather
than the move being undertaken in a positive framework. In discussion, the consensus was that it
should be possible to avoid problems of conflicting
interests and views if appropriate steps are taken
long before the situation arises. Such action
would include the fuller provision of information,

and opportunities to discuss issues with other parents and with professionals.

Chapter 12

NEEDS OF PARENTS OF ADULTS
Pauline Fairbrother

The 35 year old son of a member of my local MENCAP society died recently. Many parents of my generation, and many mentally handicapped people also, attended the funeral. Everyone, of course, was very sad, not only for the death of Peter, but for his parents in their obvious grief. But the thing that struck me most forcibly was what many parents said to me. They said how sad it was "...but...he's safe. At least John and Pat haven't got to worry about what will happen to Peter when they are gone." There was even a touch of envy in their voices. What a terrible indictment of a society that drives parents to wish that they outlive their son or daughter! We know that we can fight for their rights and protect them whilst we are alive, but we have no guarantee of what is going to happen to our children when we are no longer here.

THE FUTURE

When my daughter Diana was born 31 years ago, what was going to happen to their mentally handicapped child when they were dead was the greatest worry of all parents. It is still our greatest worry today and our biggest unsolved problem.

Parents have, in the UK, tried to help themselves. They have tried to make their son or daughter financially secure through Trusteeship and Trust schemes, but even some of these are threatened by recent government legislation. By far the best guarantee is MENCAP'S Homes Foundation, which enables parents to leave property and money and form Housing Associations that attract government and local authority funds and guarantee a place to live and people who care for their children[1]. This has the weakness that it ultimately depends to a large

extent on money being available from national and
local government sources; even then, it can only
bring security to a fairly small proportion of mentally handicapped people.

So, this most agonising problem depends always
on the support of professionals and legislators,
public money and the concern and encouragement of
the man and woman in the street.

Many countries, including the UK, have Advocacy
schemes. Advocates are trained to guard the rights
and the quality of life of those individual mentally
handicapped people who are without families. But
these advocates are volunteers, with all the disadvantages of volunteers. They cannot be ordered to
do something, many drop out for personal reasons and
we can't get enough of them to meet the need.

So none of these many schemes, good as they
are, can fully relieve parents' anxieties about the
future. Only two things can do that:

1. Existing services for education, training
    and therapy must be so good that their son
    or daughter is stretched to the limit.
2. That there is sufficient residential pro-
    vision to guarantee the most suitable
    accommodation for their son or daughter
    when it is wanted.

CHANGING POLICIES

By the time their son or daughter has reached adulthood, not only have parents gone through their early
struggles but they have had to face the hard facts
of life of adulthood: the sort of work that most
mentally handicapped people are allowed to do; the
fact that their son or daughter is never going to be
completely independent; that they themselves will
never know the fully independent life that most parents of grown-up children enjoy; that their son or
daughter will probably never marry and that there
will be no grandchildren. These are painful things
to come to terms with. But just to come to terms
with these problems is not enough: it is the point
where working together really starts. We all need
to examine our attitudes, explore new ways of looking at things and maybe change our philosophy more
quickly. If parents and professionals do this together, we may speed up the whole process of change.

It is not easy to drop one's natural protectiveness once a handicapped child grows into an adult.
We never completely achieve it; but then we continue

to feel some elements of protectiveness towards our
normal sons and daughters once they too are adults.
Nevertheless, to a greater or lesser degree, we do
manage to accept their adulthood and their need for
some independence. But we are thrown back to our
protective role if either the possibility for their
development as adults is thwarted because of attitudes or lack of training or facilities, or if we
feel that they are being pushed into situations for
which we believe they are not ready. If they are
not able to continue their education into adulthood,
if they are not able to find work in the community,
if the only place for them to lead independent lives
is in a subnormality hospital or an institutional
hostel, then we are back fighting for them, protecting them from a hostile world which rejects them.
   What areas do parents and professionals need to
explore?

The Value of Work

Firstly, we must talk about work. We live in a
society that values paid work. We value academic
achievement, monetary success and status. Work ful-
filment, developing the human being into a happy,
well adjusted, sociable person is only an after-
thought. Maybe we should start viewing work for
mentally handicapped people in this way. As education for fulfilled adulthood involves the whole
life and not just the hours spent at a training
centre or workshop, parents and professionals must
truly be partners once the philosophy is agreed
upon.

Teaching Programmes

How much should parents be involved in training
programmes whether they be physical, educational or
training towards independence? I believe that they
should only be involved if they are happy and comfortable in that involvement. They should be involved in decisions on setting goals and they should
be made aware of the methods of teaching involved.
   If speech therapy is being given, then the
family must know how and what is being taught so
that they can encourage better communication in
their everyday family life. This does not mean that
they should feel obliged to sit down every day for
half an hour doing what the speech therapist does.
If crossing roads is the skill being taught, then
the families can encourage them to try out this task
whenever they have occasion to cross a road. This
way of co-operating will not only give the mentally

handicapped person confidence, but it will give confidence to the rest of the family that he or she is
capable of mastering these skills. By giving
encouragement, parents must reinforce the training
or teaching programme in everyday life. We must not
strive so hard with parents to make them into
teachers and therapists that they have no time left
to be the one thing that they are most valuable at
doing, being parents.
     Given real co-operation, with parents feeling
comfortable and valued and equal members of the
team, then goals that are set, targets that are
aimed for must come as the result of honest discussion where in the end everyone agrees that those
goals are attainable. No parent wants to see their
offspring pushed into a situation that they feel
they cannot handle. Too often decisions are made
and training is carried on without any consultation
with the parents and quite often the parents are
left in complete ignorance of what is happening.
The parents, when they are told, may have no information which can give them confidence in their son's
or daughter's capability to achieve the goals set.
This not only makes it more difficult for the mentally handicapped person to achieve success, but also
it leaves the parents feeling helpless and frighten-
ed at the situation which is apparently out of their
control. Decisions and programme planning must be
arrived at and agreed on together.

Independence for Parents
In the past, the situation of parents and professionals preparing mentally handicapped people to lead
independent lives has rarely arisen; if parents did
keep their mentally handicapped son or daughter at
home, they usually stayed there until the parents
became incapable of caring for them or one or both
parents died. But for at least the last 20 years
there has been a growing feeling amongst parents
that they have rights. One of these rights is their
right to lead lives independent of their children
once they have become adults.
     Life becomes very restricted if you have a
mentally handicapped adult relative at home with you.
Your social life shrivels, friends stop inviting you
to visit them. Your holidays are restricted to
those suitable for your relative and your financial
situation is probably affected. Mothers find difficulty in going out to work, because problems arise
when their child is ill, or needs to go to the
doctor, the dentist, the chiropodist, the hairdresser

and the clothes shops. Life is different from the life enjoyed by your contemporaries. All this would possibly be acceptable if it truly helped the mentally handicapped person, but they know their lives are restricted also. They can not go out on their own, they are lonely. Normality for both parents and offspring is leaving the family home, seeking independence, on reaching adulthood. Parents' rights and the rights of mentally handicapped people do not conflict; they are in harmony.

I remember many years ago speaking to a group of parents about the fact that parents had rights too. An elderly mother of an adult mentally handicapped daughter came up to me, put her arms around me and started to cry. "Thank you", she said, "for saying out aloud what I had always felt, but was always guilty about having such selfish thoughts." That guilt should not be allowed to develop; however, it is often fed by well-meaning professionals and legislators. Recently, I had a letter from my Member of Parliament replying to a letter from me on the plight of mentally handicapped people in hospitals. He felt that the solution lay in the hands of parents: they should visit their children more often; they should have them home. That was adding guilt upon guilt - and this was from a responsible law maker.

The Rights of Adults
I talked earlier of the rights of mentally handicapped people and parents being in harmony. But sometimes the fact that they are really similar is not recognised by parents because the parents have not understood, for a variety of reasons, that they should be part of the team. The only right that they are interested in is the right to protect their mentally handicapped son or daughter. As a result of this attitude the mentally handicapped person's rights may be being denied. This situation must obviously not be allowed to continue and the rights of the mentally handicapped person must take priority and be jealously guarded. But it must always be recognised that the reasons behind the attitude of the parents are rarely selfish or deliberately obstructive. Their attitudes have grown out of love for their son or daughter. It is quite likely that professionals have not approached them in the right way, and have not taken their feelings and anxieties into account. We must never give up seeking their co-operation and approval and support, even if for the moment, decisions have to be taken contrary

to the wishes of the parents. But we must be absol-
utely sure, before such a drastic step is taken,
that if we did not take that step more harm would be
done to the mentally handicapped person concerned
than the harm that will be done by flouting the
parents' wishes.

Sexual Needs
It is time for us to talk together about the sexual
needs of mentally handicapped people. Parents have
many anxieties about these needs. But because both
parents and professionals are human beings with
sexual experiences and sexual attitudes, good and
bad, discussions on this subject should be on a
truly equal basis. It will not be productive if
professionals call a meeting of parents to discuss
the parents' attitudes, and intend just to help the
parents. Professional attitudes needs to be examined also.
    Discussions on sexual attitudes and needs have
to be planned carefully. Small groups in relaxing
surroundings are essential. I believe that the best
person to lead the discussion is a parent, preferably a mother, because a parent can say things to
both parents and professionals that will not be rejected by either on the grounds of, "What does he/
she know about it?" I also believe that a parent
can talk about sex with more warmth and humour. A
professional, because of his or her profession, has
to view it more clinically and with less humour.
Sexual intercourse is only a part of our sexual
needs. We should discuss what we believe are the
sexual needs of severely mentally handicapped people
whom we know and the relationships which they form.
Perhaps we can then modify or better still banish
some of our fears that every kiss and cuddle will
inevitably lead to bed and sexual intercourse.
    Do we allow relationships to develop or do we
intervene because, in our judgement, they are unsuitable relationships, or we are worried because of
what they might lead to? Remember that we are talking about people who, because of the severity of
their handicap, are never alone. They are never
allowed to pursue close personal relationships, because they need to be alone with the other person
for this relationship to flourish. How often are
they allowed to learn how to relate to other people,
to make mistakes and to learn from them? How often
have we said on seeing two people petting," I know
that it is nice, but not on the coach (or at the club
or in the workshop). It is not socially acceptable"

(or words to that effect)? Do we ever ask ourselves
where and when it *is* socially acceptable? What are
people's sexual rights?

We need to discuss marriage between severely
mentally handicapped people and their having children. Have they ever been exposed to the reality of
a baby or have they a starry-eyed view on babies?
If they are not, in our opinion, capable of independent living and the responsibilities of marriage,
are they then to be excluded from loving, intimate
relationships?

Finally, we must discuss how we should help
mentally handicapped people understand their bodies,
their emotions and their relationships.

Helping mentally handicapped people understand
and develop their sexuality should be a joint programme. Parents and professionals have distinctive
and separate roles to fulfill, but these roles will
only be fulfilled if they are carefully worked for
together.

Death and Bereavement
One further thing that we need to talk about together and help each other about is death. We
handle it very badly with mentally handicapped
people. We don't prepare them for the death of
people whom they love. We shut them out from mourn-
ing because we think we are protecting them from
hurt. Very often, with the sudden death of a parent
comes, for the first time, removal to an institution
or hostel, a strange place with strange people.

The subject of death can, like sex, be very
painful to talk about. In discussing both topics it
is necessary to look at our own feelings first and
then to look at the problem in relation to mentally
handicapped people.

Preparing mentally handicapped people for the
death of their parents must mean preparing them for
living an independent life. To lead an independent
life they must have training, they must have a ful-
filling occupation, they must be able to satisfy
their sexual needs and, most important, they must
have a suitable place to live.

That brings me back to where I started. The
overwhelming need of parents is for a guarantee of
security for their sons or daughters. Until parents
have that guarantee they will go on wishing to outlive their mentally handicapped son or daughter.

CONCLUSION

Parents need to feel that all they have learned from
having a mentally handicapped son or daughter, all
the years of experience, all the years of achieving
professionalism have not been wasted, that they are
recognised and used. Parents, particularly of adult
mentally handicapped people, have a lot to offer, on
equal terms with other professionals. Frequently
only lip service is paid to the parents' role in the
team. I recently heard a paediatrician stating that
when parents are invited to talk about their child
with the professional team, the team, after discussing the case in private, should break up into standing, chatting groups before the parents are invited
it. In this way the parents will not come into an
already-seated group and will feel more at ease as
they all take their seats together. Why was all
this necessary? Why were they discussing the child
without the parents being present? That is giving
the lie to their stated belief that parents are an
important, some say the most important, part of the
team.
        Parents and professionals can only give
strength to each other through mutual respect and a
spirit of true equality.

NOTES

        1.   Information on all these schemes can be
obtained from MENCAP, 123 Golden Lane, London
EC1Y ORT.

DISCUSSION

In discussion, Pauline Fairbrother reaffirmed the
potential value of the experience and skills of parents of adult mentally handicapped people both for
professionals and for parents of younger children.
Many parents want to share their experiences and to
feel that their knowledge can be used in planning
services, in solving practical problems and in
giving emotional support to others. Sharing the
information they have gathered can benefit themselves too, feeling that they are contributing to
today's better services rather than feeling bitter
that they did not have such provision when their own
child was growing up.
        There was considerable discussion of the diffi-
culties in realising a 'normal' life-style for mentally handicapped adults. Pauline Fairbrother felt

that the concept of 'normalisation' required much greater discussion than at present between professionals and parents in order to avoid the adoption of inappropriate aims. For example, 'normalisation' should not result in highly abnormal pressures on parents and siblings, nor should the handicapped person be made unhappy.

Mentally handicapped people have, as any other adults do, a right to independence and privacy; a right to choose eg. what to wear or where to go on holiday; and a need to be away from their parents at least some of the time. But on the other hand, they need help to achieve these things. In many cases, the skills required to cope with the everyday demands of living in the community can be taught, if there is cooperation between parents and professionals and if a relatively consistent environment is provided in which to exercise these skills.

However, parents very often are uneasy about the idea of their son or daughter living away from home. Philippa Russell pointed out that it will mean a change in, and perhaps a loss, of close relationships for both the handicapped person and the other members of the family. Henri Bissonnier raised the question of how the relationship between the family and residential care staff (of whatever level of supervisory responsibility) is managed, and how the responsibilities of the family are conceptualised in the case of an adult mentally handicapped person.

Parents' reluctance to 'put their child away' may arise from a lack of suitable alternative provision, from a lack of information about alternatives (eg. hostels, group homes), or from a deeply felt moral obligation to care for the handicapped person for as long as possible. The phrase 'putting him/her away' is still often used by parents in discussing the subject. Dorothy Jeffree stated that most parents of teenagers interviewed by the PATH project also rejected short-term care, even if offered simply as preparation for a future time when the parents would no longer be alive. Some parents except or have arranged that another of their children will take over the care of the mentally handicapped person, although the sibling may have promised while not really welcoming the responsibilities.

Ensuring that families have information about alternatives, and real choice, will greatly improve the chances of mentally handicapped people being able to live as fully in accordance with their potentialities as possible.

SECTION SIX: DISCUSSION AND FOLLOW-UP

Chapter 13

EXAMPLES OF PARTNERSHIP IN EUROPE

Helen McConachie

LANGUAGE AND PERSPECTIVES

Fundamental to the rationale for the European Seminar was the appreciation that participants from different countries would approach our discussion from a variety of perspectives. In learning of others' experiences, we would be enabled to see our own more clearly. Our discussion revealed interesting differences in past and current relationships between professionals and parents of handicapped children and several participants wrote vivid accounts of their experiences. This chapter is drawn from those experiences.

Gugu Kristoffersen from *Denmark* directly tackled the issues underlying how differing experiences are described, ie. how we perceive our experiences and how we describe them through the imperfect medium of language. An appreciation of such issues helps to clarify some of the ways in which parents and professionals may fail to communicate even when attempting to do so.

"When preparing myself for the seminar I had piles of books and articles around me, and I thought to myself how much has been written and discussed, and how experts of various kinds have shared their information.

The very first seminar I attended ten years ago was the International League of Societies for the Mentally Handicapped Seminar in Copenhagen on "Cooperation between parents and staff". Another report arrived just days ago, a UNESCO report on *Early Detection, Intervention and Education*. In the years in between, transdisciplinary initiatives have produced hundreds of pages of *words, words, words*. I thought to myself, will *we* manage to boil down our experiences to a few crystal clear sentences, worth passing on to politicians, parents, care-workers, the public - and will one or two ideas inspire researchers?

We parents need research badly: sometimes statistics can persuade politicians. When mothers are actively speaking or writing, their messages are seen through a stereotype of the mother-child bond that to most people will mean not only love, but mercy and overprotection. What do professionals think of parents? I think an investigation would show a colourful picture and, I am sad to say, not a very true picture. An active parent is often not listened to, dismissed with 'She is not typical!' I would like to see some research in this area.

As family patterns and constellations change, it is important for us to be particularly open to what is happening in society. *The last to enjoy progress in a society are handicapped persons.* One present trend is that women want to 'realize themselves' - maybe fewer mothers want to stay at home. Also the economic situation is such that the family cannot exist on one person's salary. We need to discuss these issues when considering home-visiting services.

Another trend in society is that fathers are being drawn into the lives of little children much more than before. It is generally accepted that fathers are present at the birth of their children, that they take part to a greater extent in the changing of nappies, playing, feeding etc. This trend is a good trend which will benefit handicapped children also - and mothers.

Some even suggest that this trend will make itself felt in political decisions in times to come; in questions about war and peace; in higher priorities for families with children, for kids on bicycles in comparison with motorways, etc.

I would like to explore the problem of language. We use a lot of words, but are we talking about the same things? We must choose our words and make sure we are being understood. For example, how do we pass on research results in plain language to those who need the information? We must make 'translations', rewrite and perhaps rediscover. Researchers need a dialogue with parents who can contribute greatly with examples from their experience, etc. Both parties will understand more.

Personally, I feel torn between my usual colourful subjective way of expressing myself as a mother, and the dull, cool, objective way I struggle to learn and use for reports as a student of education.

An even greater language problem is that of
professional *secrecy*. If we do not share information,
we cannot cooperate. If the care-worker knows
everything about me, and I know nothing about him or
her, it will never be a genuine, relaxed cooperation. Parents are sensitive to professional
jealousy. Professionals have their different roles,
but parents have no uniform, no set role. They are
problem-solvers, and so are part parents, and part
social workers, care-workers, physiotherapists,
speech therapists. Thus, they have difficulty in
understanding the fencing-in of little parts of the
problem.

As a practical example of exploring roles and
language, I have often asked for parent instructors
at training-colleges for care-workers - not just a
parent asked to give a lecture once a year on a
certain topic, but parents' perspectives reflected
in every part of the curriculum.

Also, in Denmark, there is a growing awareness
of the problems of guest workers' families. How can
we identify children who need help early? How do we
overcome language and religious barriers, ignorance,
discrimination? Practical, social and cultural
problems piled on top of each other.

When looking at early stimulation, it is
important to see the first two or three years in
perspective. They are part of the whole, crucial
not only for the child but also for the lifelong
attitudes of the parents and for any later co-
operation with the services. For fifteen years I
have been tackling problems essential to the understanding of early stimulation: *early* stimulation of
parents, of children, of staff; *eternal* stimulation of
politicians and the public."

EARLY INTERVENTION

Our discussion in the seminar of what kinds of early
help are most appropriate for children and for
families was furthered by hearing about a *Belgian*
example of close cooperation between parents and a
professional. *Lucienne van Loon* described the centre
for early support to families with preschool mentally handicapped children in which she works with
Claudine van Malderen, who also attended the Seminar.

"In contrast to most of the existing services,
our centre was started by parents, all members of
the National Association for the Mentally Handicapped, who already met as a self-support group.
Although we largely succeeded in helping parents,

we gradually became aware that to attempt to meet all needs, we had to engage a professional (Claudine van Malderen, a 'pedagogue'). Unfortunately, being the first ones to start a service centre in this way has meant that, up to now, we have not had any government funds, and we work on a voluntary basis. However, in the near future, similar service centres will be set up all over the country, and recent contact with the government has led us to hope that they will be state-aided.

We started our centre four years ago, and during that period well over seventy families have attended. Our team is composed of the pedagogue and a so-called 'key-parent'. The reason why we included a parent in the team is that no one can sympathize with parents of a handicapped child as well as another parent of a handicapped child. We have had the same griefs, the same disappointments, the same guilt feelings, the same negative feelings towards our child. I can assure you that it gives great relief to talk freely with a fellow parent about those emotions and to realize at the same time that you are not the only one to have them. In addition, the newly affected parents can learn from the key-parent's experiences with her own child and especially that, although life with a handicapped child has problems, these are not so insuperable as it seems at first.

The early intervention we provide aims to meet the specific needs of each family. Therefore, we offer several kinds of help:

- emotional support;
- realistic and genuine information about the handicap;
- documentation;
- information about other existing services;
- early intervention programmes;
- educational advice;
- information about social rights and help in getting allowances.

Thus, we offer a choice of services for the parents, the handicapped child and the siblings, but we never force them to make use of any of them. Our experience has shown that each family has its specific needs, expectations and problems and does not necessarily make use of all the offered services.

When families visit the centre, the key-parent welcomes them and makes them feel at ease as much as possible and also tries to be a link between them.

208

while they all chat together and drink a cup of coffee, each family in its turn visits the pedagogue in a separate consulting-room. Ms van Malderen evaluates the child's development, using standardized tests. The parents have a great deal to contribute to making the assessment, by giving information about their child. According to the results, Ms van Malderen explains what is to be expected as the next step forward in the child's total development and she demonstrates how the parents can stimulate the child by playing adapted games. At the same time she stresses the meaning and the importance of the games, so that the parents are motivated to play at home with the child. She also writes down notes so that the parents can easily remember what was suggested. We feel it is very valuable in encouraging positive attitudes in the parents for the professional to play in an enthusiastic way with the child. During the consultation, which usually lasts between one and one and a half hours Ms van Malderen will also invite the parents to talk about other problems, for example, difficulties with siblings.

Our first aim is that parents should be reassured that they can cope with the education of their handicapped child. The interval between consultations is fixed in such a way that each time parents can see progress in development of the child. Apart from the consultations, the parents are always welcome to drop in for a chat, and they can also ring us at any time. After the child has gone to school, parents can still call upon us whenever they need to.

We have chosen to have a team of one professional and one key-parent for each family in order to create a confidential relationship which will help to establish a clear view of the family's special needs and problems. The importance of the key-parent is evidenced in the kinds of questions parents ask her; meeting other parents increases "comfort, solidarity, practical advice and general support" (Russell, Chapter 2, this volume). Besides the working of the centre, the association provides parent contacts in organizing play-groups for the children, discussion groups, conferences with a guest speaker, etc.

We are well aware that we cannot solve all the problems. When specific therapies are indicated, we introduce the parents to professionals of another discipline. By preference we suggest professionals who accept the parents as co-educators."

STRUCTURE OF SERVICES

The Belgian parents' group had challenged the usual
structure of services by being the ones to hire the
professional worker. Other ways in which parents
have influenced services into becoming more responsive to individual families' situations were described by *Erica Lund* and *Henrik Pelling* from *Sweden*.

"Parents' organizations have influenced the
creation of new forms of cooperation between professionals and parents. The earlier form of centering attention around mothers has been widened to include fathers. Very often this type of cooperation
can be created when both parents, and to a certain
degree even brothers and sisters, take part in receiving information after the handicap has first
been diagnosed. When the first crisis has become a
general concern for *all* family members, it will be
easier for every one to participate in caring for
the handicapped child. A division of labour where
the mother mainly takes care of the handicapped
child, and the father concentrates on helping the
brothers and sisters, can naturally function well
in many cases, but the model can show itself to be
weak, since the mother is a bit too alone in her
involvement in a very difficult task.

Every individual and every family is unique,
and therefore it is important that contacts be
limited to a few professionals who get to know the
family well. Organized parent groups for different
types of handicap have together influenced the coordination of the various facilities of the society.
A special organization entitled 'child habilitation'
is being developed at present for this purpose. In
this organization each family will have a 'contact' person whose main role will be to support the
family, coordinate resources, and help as an inter-
mediary, in terms of information from different experts. This 'contact' person can belong to any of
several occupational groups: physical therapists,
psychologists, social workers, for example. In this
way it will be easier for the specialists to concentrate on their own tasks, be it speech therapy,
medical help etc. The 'contact' person will be able
to help the specialists cooperate among themselves,
as it is he or she who is most able to survey the
individual family's needs and resources."

PARENTAL RELUCTANCE?

The description of the Belgian parents' group

aroused great interest, particularly as several seminar participants cited 'parental reluctance' as an obstacle in the way of creating partnership. For example, *Bob van Zijderveld* described the situation in the *Netherlands*.

"In preparation for the seminar, two meetings were held of a small group of parents and professionals. Our impression is that in Holland parents do not often become involved in systematic educational programmes. Dutch families seem to be concerned in the first place with providing their children with security and a warm emotional climate in the home and family (ideally, that is!). They are not very eager to become involved in the education of their children in day-centres, kindergartens and schools. For example, a mother told a social worker she was afraid to answer the telephone, because it might be the day-centre asking her to join a coffee-morning. Apparently, parents often do not like the confrontation with other handicapped children, and see their own situation as unique.

It is our experience that parents in Holland are less interested than parents in Britain and some other countries in contributing directly to what they consider to be the field of professionals: they leave to the professionals responsibility for the development of educational programmes. They expect the experts to know the solution to any problem, to train the child and to work systematically on its psychological education."

The Dutch description of parental lack of involvement in educational programmes was couched mainly in terms of parents' personal emotional feelings. However *Sonja Barthel*, a teacher from *West Germany*, saw the issue more in terms of traditional attitudes toward the teacher's role.

"For parents, professionals generally signify 'authority'. When they were children the teacher was a person to be obeyed and never contradicted. The expectations parents have of a teacher's role are generally associated with 'performance' or 'achievement'. Can this attitude be changed? Do teachers always want to be looked on as an authority? Do they make excessive demands on their pupils?

In my experience, it is not the teachers who do this, but the parents! The majority of parents are of the opinion that their child should have at least as good a life as they do, that their sort of standard of living can only be reached by way of a good education, and that this can only be obtained with the aid of the teacher. In principle, parents by-pass the abilities and needs of the child when they take this attitude."

Christoph Hublow, also from *West Germany*, balanced this description by stressing the influence of teachers' traditional attitudes towards parents that teachers have the answer to every question whether or not they have been asked. He also expanded the point about the nature of parental expectations of 'a good education'.

"German parents generally tend to put very great emphasis on their children's learning the '3 Rs', whereas they do not fully acknowledge the value of practical skills. In the case of severely handicapped children, who are really unable to learn any abstract skills, cooperation between teachers and parents may become very difficult."

He also raised the point that many parents - perhaps tending to be the younger, more progressive ones - are now reluctant to cooperate with special schools, "despite the fact that these schools were founded and established according to and because of parents' wishes and concepts, 10 or 20 years ago. They argue that special schools hinder the process of social integration of handicapped children, and are convinced that their children could learn more if they were allowed to go to normal schools. Many of them refer to the Italian school-system "(which become fully integrated in 1975).

Thus, rather than parents being 'reluctant', they may in fact be asserting a different viewpoint from professionals on their children's education. The *Swedish* participants also challenged professional assumptions that parents should be heavily involved in their children's education.

"Voluntary organizations in Sweden have succeeded in making society responsible for support and aid, which for each handicapped child should mean that he or she receives the greatest opportunity possible to be integrated into normal life. In practical terms, this means integration in schools, integration in ordinary living areas, supplemented with the necessary supervision, and adoption of places of work for the handicapped. When these measures are taken, there is a less negative influence on the social life of the family with a handicapped child.

One important thing is that direct parental assistance in treatment or training programmes in nursery schools, regular schools, boarding schools etc. is no longer necessary. Instead, parents have

212

the freedom to choose how much time they wish to
spend on their child's training programme and day-
care. In essence, the parents' responsibility for
training of new abilities has now been transferred
to professionals. The parents' task is to provide
the best possible environment in a socially intact
family, in which the handicapped child can best use
his or her new abilities."

Several of the themes described above as contributing to difficulties in the relationship
between parents and teachers – parents' seeing education as solely the responsibility of teachers,
fear of challenging authority, placing high value on
academic skills – were clearly illustrated in the
history of a *German* working partnership presented by
Sonja Barthel and Renate Börner, from which extracts are
given below.

PARENT AND TEACHER

Renate Börner's son, Andreas, contracted a virus in-
infection at the age of 15 months and suffered brain
damage as a result.

"From the beginning I took part in physical and
speech training exercises with Andreas and found out
myself how severe his handicap was and what an
effort he had to make. When he entered the preliminary class of the special school for educationally
subnormal children, I was very disappointed with
the type of education he received. In the class 25
children, ranging from those with mild to those with
severe learning difficulties, were given two hours
of instruction daily. The teaching involved only
academic skills. The children had to sit at desks
and write out numbers and letters of the alphabet.
It was frightful. One girl with Down's syndrome
copied out English texts, although she could neither
talk nor recognise any of the letters. Some of the
children were hyperactive, and for them having to
sit still was next to impossible. Every one of the
children showed uneasiness, evidenced in such behaviours as burying their heads in their arms or
hanging on the doorpost so as not to have to enter
the classroom.

The teacher was quite unable to meet our
queries and reservations with understanding. He
perceived our concerns as an attack on his authority. As a group of those united by the same fate,
we parents eventually found the strength to do
something about the unsatisfactory conditions.

Together with some of the staff from the local

Teacher Training College, we founded an action group to set up a remedial facility, and had 24 children tested to assess their mental handicap, and to establish their claim to a different form of schooling. By 1972 we had reached our goal and 55 children entered the new facility. During the time in which the facility was being built, we had worked out a conceptual basis for the children's instruction with the college staff, teachers and 'educators'. ('Educators' have trained to work in kindergartens; in special schools they generally teach social, musical and practical skills.)

As a result of the good liaison within the group, the discussions, the frankly stated opinions and the bad experience with schooling which lay behind us, we decided that no academic skills would initially be taught in the day facility, although some parents found this decision difficult to accept. My son had been attending a Rudolf Steiner boarding school in southern Germany, and I participated in the life of his school and the instruction there for two or three days every four weeks. However, after some years, he increasingly expressed the desire to live at home with his brothers and sisters. As we missed him just as much, we decided to bring him home again, where he joined Frau Barthel's class."

Sonja Barthel gave us an account of her experiences as a teacher up to this time. She had taught in a school for educationally subnormal children, and then moved to the school for mentally handicapped children. As a trained teacher, she came under pressure from parents' expectations that their children would acquire academic skills.

"As I had never worked with children with an IQ under 60 before, I took over the parents' expectations and tried to build up a system which would allow the children to recognise words and letters and to understand and reproduce them. Slowly and with a good deal of effort some of the children did manage to recognise letters of the alphabet. However, as progress was so slow, the parents made it clear to me that the children should also have homework. Although I did not think it was necessary, as the children were at school from 8 a.m. until 3 p.m., and often had an hour's travelling time, I did give them homework. Interest in learning new things dropped off considerably in some children, until I found out that the parents were treating their handicapped children as they did their other children; for instance, pages of work which had been completed would be torn up and had to be written or painted again, because they were not 'neat' or 'tidy' enough.

In the meantime, however, I had begun to have insight into the ability of each child in my class. I began discussions with the parents, and, unfortunately, I found myself in the same frustrating position as that in which I had been with the parents in other schools. Only a few of them were able to see me as an equal partner. The image of the teacher which they had assumed in their childhood prevented them from seeing me as anything other than an 'authority'. The meetings usually ended with the parents' accepting my observations and suggestions without comment, although I noticed that there were things that they were not really happy about. Many of them considered that their children had a greater ability to learn than I described. To a certain extent they were right, for each child in my class had practical abilities and could in some way or other be approached by way of musical activities. Many a child who could hardly speak could find his or her way around the town and the shops, and enjoyed weaving, painting or handicrafts. My aim was to foster these abilities, but, sadly, this was not enough for many parents; the 'tools of culture' were more important to them.

I then had a piece of luck in that the child of one of the founders of our institution joined my class. The broadmindedness of Andreas's mother, who accepts her son's handicap, and recognises his limits, helped the other parents in the class to see their children as they are and not as they would like them to be. Frau Börner encouraged parents to visit the classes and take part in educational walks, etc. This means that the parents experience their child in the community with the others in the class, and, as a result, they are much more able to accept his or her capabilities.

It was natural for Frau Börner and me to discuss everything we noticed about Andreas, whether it was positive or negative. Together we tried to find ways to build up the positive aspects and minimise the negative ones."

Renate Börner then described the next stages in the life of the school.

"In our class group of mothers (fathers usually were occupied elsewhere), teacher and educators, there was a frank and friendly atmosphere. In some groups, however, the atmosphere was no longer good, because the teachers had assumed too great an influence.

This started to develop in 1976, when it became obligatory for mentally handicapped children to attend school. (In the West German federal system, different parts of the country organize school-systems differently, and brought in a compulsory education law at different times.) The teachers, who had previously been paid by the Ministry for Social Affairs, took a second examination after some time, and were then employed by the Ministry of Education as teachers in special schools for the mentally handicapped. We wished to see a continuation of our model, drawn from experience, that teachers and educators have equally important roles to play in the training of the children.

Sadly, the new kind of school, which is, by law, more tightly organised than before, led to the teachers gaining the upper hand. There was no more equality; the educators increasingly took on the role of assistants. As a result the parents fell back into their usual behaviour towards school - the teacher is an authority, only addressed when problems crop up, one does not dare to discuss anything, because the teacher, being an expert, knows everything better anyway. The frank and easy 'general assembly' was replaced by the School Conference. As a result, the parents were intimidated and conversations at an equal level were no longer possible.

Frequently the newly arrived teachers did not understand how easily parents of handicapped children, living, as they often do, in permanently over-taxing conditions, can be made to feel unsure of themselves and also feel guilty when the children do not meet the demands made on them.

In summary, it can be said that cooperation between parents and professionals has become more difficult to implement since the new school system was introduced.

If more favourable conditions, such as those Andreas enjoyed, are to be maintained, teachers must recognise that parents of handicapped children need more time and understanding than others do. It is important actually to include them in the instruction the child receives in practical, social and musical skills. This is certainly unusual and requires many meetings with parents, not just the conventional single parents' visit in the year. It means being able to listen, and to take up and work on the observations made by parents and educators.

It is only when teachers learn these - at

216

present unconventional – forms of interaction, and when parents grow to understand that, owing to their daily experience with their children, they are themselves experts and certainly have a right to participate equally in the 'schooling' of their children, that a genuine partnership between parents and professionals can result."

Another team of parent and teacher, *Berit Rohmen and Kari Storemyr*, came from *Norway*. They described the ways in which parental involvement in special schools is formally structured there.

"Cooperation between teachers and parents in liaison committees is authorized by law, and every school must establish such a committee. It includes two parents, two teachers, the headteacher, one pupil, one member of the non-teaching staff and one member appointed by the community education authority. The committee's work includes advice and recommendations on the school budget, on educational subjects and on other matters concerning the school society. A subcommittee consisting of three members elected amongst the parents is responsible for arranging meetings, leisure activities like skiing, and other events and projects of a social and informative character."

Kari Storemyr, a teacher in a 6o-pupil school, then described how she works with the parents of her pupils.

"I have to arrange two group meetings a year with parents of children in my class. These are usually in the evening and we talk about the curriculum for the year and about the class in general. Twice a year I write reports to the parents about the child, where the main content is the child's progress and social functioning at school. The form of record is the same which we use in school in order to follow up the child.

Twice a year we also arrange case conferences, where the whole staff of professionals is assembled. Parents are not allowed to take part in the conferences, and they do not receive a record of them. However, parents have questioned this, and we are currently discussing including the parents, which I hope will happen soon.

One hour a week is set aside for conferring with parents about matters of mutual concern. I also contact parents regularly by telephone, letters, visits, home-school notebooks and homework.

During each year, I have two meetings at school with each set of parents to discuss the child's work and progress. I feel that I am succeeding in my

217

efforts to build a relationship of trust with most of the parents. We are becoming friends and are able to communicate even if we have different opinions. But it depends, of course, on the parents being willing to collaborate. Collaboration is of great value when parent and teacher work on an equal footing, trying to stimulate the child from different angles.

In Norway, discussion similar to elsewhere is going on, around the argument that the education of handicapped children is highly skilled and has to be carried out by specially trained staff. I agree with this point of view, but stress that active inclusion of parents can enhance the educational opportunities of our children. I regard parent involvement as a necessary part of the total school situation."

Erica Lund and Henrik Pelling echoed their Scandinavian neighbours in stressing the value of parents' and teachers' differing roles, and suggested very positive reasons for this recent emphasis.

"Clearer roles, more detailed and defined, make professionals more aware that parents are specialists at taking care of their particular handicapped child in their family. The reason for more clearly defined roles amongst professional groups such as teachers in special education, physical therapists, psychologists and physicians is largely due to better education. When they are being trained for their respective occupations, they receive more information concerning handicaps, both theoretical and practical. Parents in organized parent groups, because they have received better help from professionals, have been able to place emphasis on the most important question concerning their roles - this question is: 'How can my family, in the best possible way, take care of all family members, including those who are handicapped?'"

ADOLESCENTS AND ADULTS

The two participants from *France, Henri Bissonnier* and *Yvonne de Laval*, made some observations about services after school-age for mentally handicapped people which suggested that immediate needs may have been met there more adequately than in many other countries. Mentally handicapped young people may attend Centres d'Aide par Travail (C.A.T.) which were set up as a preliminary step towards a sheltered workshop, but which do not themselves have a work output, nor do they include specific training. A

problem of transfer to sheltered workshops has
arisen in that there are now very few of the latter
for severely mentally handicapped people. Instituts
Medico-Professionels (I.M.Pro.) provide training in
fundamental skills for more able mentally handicapped people up to the age of about 20 years. They
are then expected to find work in ordinary jobs;
there is a legal quota system to aid handicapped
people in gaining employment in France. Other
possible avenues on leaving school include Occupational Homes, and weekly Boarding Schools for
severely mentally handicapped young people aged 16
to 21 years. All of these options give handicapped
adolescents opportunities to meet peers and to make
friends. In addition the Franco-American Volunteers
Association organizes integrated youth clubs and
sports activities.

A feature of these services is group discussion
between parents and staff, who aim to understand and
try to help with the particular problems of this age
group. For example, adolescence may be the time
when young people become acutely aware of their
handicap and its vocational consequences, and they
may need help to develop, retain and bolster their
sense of self-respect. In certain respects, they
will be truly adolescent, for example in developing
sexual interests, and yet at the same time remain
'childish' in cognitive levels and play interests.
Relations with brothers and sisters may become
strained, if they are younger and yet are allowed
greater independence.

As well as supportive discussion, families
will often welcome the opportunity for positive
activities. In France, groups of mentally handicapped adults and their families meet on Sundays
with young people and other families, meeting as
friends to do things together, not *for* the handicapped person.

In France, a greater proportion than in Britain
of mentally handicapped adults are in some kind of
residential accommodation, away from their families'
homes. Professor Bissonnier laid stress on the
problems of expecting siblings to look after a
mentally handicapped brother or sister. "This must
generally be considered as too heavy a burden for
them, particularly when the siblings marry and have
their own children. Furthermore, it is not always
suitable nor reasonable for a mentally handicapped
adult to belong, like a child, to an older or even a
younger brother or sister. 'Looking after' must
instead be understood as having the commitment to

protect and to defend the rights and interests of
the handicapped person, not necessarily taking
charge of him or her in their own home." The
question then arises of how this commitment, and the
relationship with care staff, can be best facilitated.

CONCLUSION

The contrasting viewpoints speak for themselves. A
strong feeling emerged from the discussion that so
many important questions were being raised by our
comparing experiences and perspectives that such a
Seminar should be perhaps only the first of many.
We also realised that our knowledge of and ideas
about partnership between professionals and parents
of young children were greatly in advance of our
understanding of the issues and our knowledge of
current examples in the case of adolescents and
adult mentally handicapped people. Our planning for
the future is described in the next chapter.

REFERENCES

United Nations Educational Scientific and Cultural
    Organisation (1980) Handicapped Children:
    Early Detection, Intervention and Education.
    (ED/MD/63) Paris: UNESCO

Chapter 14

PLANNING FOR FUTURE DEVELOPMENTS

Peter Mittler

ACTION SEMINARS

A seminar or conference is only as good as the results that spring from it. But all too often, this
is left to chance on the assumption that ideas which
have been stimulated by what has been heard either
in the conference or - more often perhaps - in social encounters outside the formal sessions themselves, will somehow lead to new developments. On
this occasion, the seminar organisers made it clear
at the time when invitations were first issued that
participants would be asked to do everything possible to work for short term goals relevant to parent-
professional collaboration in their own countries,
and were asked to think from the outset about ways
in which they might contribute to this, either as
single individuals or in pairs. They were also asked to make suggestions for improvements in parent-
professional relationships, either in their own
country or elsewhere, whether or not these formed
part of their own personal plans.
   The notion of using conferences and seminars as
a catalyst for the development of a local initiative
is beginning to be considered at both national and
international levels. In contrast to meetings where
people come together mainly to listen to 'experts'
or to discuss amongst themselves, the conference is
deliberately organised and planned from the outset
in such a way that participants can plan some form
of implementation after they return to their own
communities.
   Such a model was used in a recent workshop organised in Hong Kong by the International League of
Societies for Persons with Mental Handicap (ILSMH)
with support from the United Nations Fund created
within the framework of the International Year of

Disabled Persons. Thirteen countries from the Asian region were invited to nominate teams of three people - a parent of a mentally handicapped child, a teacher/educator and a community worker. An intensive five day workshop was held in which participants first shared ideas and experiences about their own situations but then worked almost entirely in small groups practising specific methods and techniques of assessment and individual programme planning relevant to teaching handicapped children basic skills, such as movement, activities for daily living and self-care, language and communication and socially appropriate behaviour. A prerequisite for being selected for the workshop was that each 'national team' undertook to develop a realistic goal plan which would lead to measurable improvements in some aspect of their local situation. These goal plans were listed and publicly discussed at the end of the workshop; the extent to which they are actually implemented is being investigated by an independent evaluator who will keep in touch with participants and will visit most of them in their own communities, with the help of funds specially provided for this purpose by the UN (see Mittler and Beasley, 1982, for a full report).

At national level in the U.K., the King's Fund and the Association of Professions for the Mentally Handicapped have held a number of 'action seminars', in which small groups come together to identify a problem, prepare and discuss an action plan for implementation in their own localities and then reconvene some months later in order to share ideas and experiences on their successes and failures. In this way, small teams from different parts of the country can benefit from one another's experiences. Such an approach may help to make conferences and seminars more productive and 'cost effective' at a time when the world-wide economic recession is making it increasingly difficult to organise and fund both international and national conferences.

Accordingly, the final session of the seminar was devoted to a general discussion in which participants briefly discussed their own plans and listed other suggestions which they wished to make. This chapter summarises the plans and the suggestions, but also extends the discussion by considering a number of wider issues concerned with the theme of partnership and lists a number of ways in which the relationships between parents and professionals can be enhanced, as well as some of the obstacles which may impede progress.

GOAL PLANS

Plans reported by participants took a variety of forms, and were quite properly a reflection of individual needs and local priorities. What is possible in one community is not necessarily realistic in another. It was emphasised that the plans should be capable of realisation in a short period of time and that the degree to which the plans had been implemented should be objectively measurable. For example, plans to 'modify professional attitudes' cannot easily be judged in terms of outcome, unless quite concrete or specific criteria for evaluation can be specified - in which case it would surely be better to select these as goal plans in the first place.

The basic ingredient of a 'goal plan' is that a specific target for action should be identified, so that it would be a relatively simple matter to determine whether or not the target had been attained. For example, several teams agreed to write an article on what they had learned from the seminar or to give talks to both parents and professional associations on a relevant subject. Here again, as some participants found, it is one thing to write an article, quite another to have it accepted for publication.

A second essential element of a goal plan is that it should include an action plan setting out a step-by-step programme on how the goal is to be reached. If, for example, the goal is to form a parent-teacher association at a school, the first step for a parent might be to arrange an appointment with the headteacher to discuss the subject. Some tasks need only one step - e.g. making a telephone call - others may require a number of steps, some of which may in turn require breaking down into even smaller steps if they cannot be achieved in one operation.

Another element of a goal plan involves the drawing up of a list of 'strengths' - i.e. the resources which are already available. These might include one or more like-minded people who can help in reaching the desired outcome; it can include the availability of existing policies - for example, a school may already have formally adopted a policy of working more closely with parents; but it can also include one's own personal qualities, even one's determination to secure a particular goal.

There are obvious parallels between the drawing up of an individual goal plan for a particular handicapped student and the development of a goal plan for the attainment of a particular objective for a service or for part of a service. In each case, there needs to be a clear statement of *who* will do *what, when,* under what *circumstances* and with what *help,* and with what *result* - i.e. how can it be known for certain whether the goal has been achieved? (For guidance on goal planning, see Georgiades and Phillimore, 1975; Houts and Scott, 1975; Blunden and Revill, 1980.)

Exploring and Meeting Local Needs
Many participants felt stimulated and encouraged to explore ways in which better relationships between parents and professionals could be developed in their own local settings. One common way of initiating discussions which was felt to be promising was to call a meeting to report verbally on the seminar, to translate or distribute at least some of the pre-circulated papers, summarise the discussions and to highlight particular points or examples of collaboration which might be taken up at local level.

One deputy head teacher decided to call a series of parents' meetings to share ideas on ways in which parents might like to be more involved in the life of the school; she noted that parents were often more willing to help in 'normal' activities, such as sports days, school outings, and to lend a hand with skills they already had; moreover, some parents needed help with transport and baby sitting.

Another suggestion was that schools might write down their present policies and practice with respect to parent-professional relationships and use this as a basis for discussion between parents and school staff on how they could work more productively together in the future.

In Manchester, the School Psychological and Child Guidance Service had just begun to develop a questionnaire for each of the City's 28 special schools in which many specific elements of collaboration were listed. The results of this questionnaire have now been analysed (Mittler, H., 1982) and are being fed back to the schools, to the parents and to other organisations. It is of particular interest that administration of the questionnaire interview itself appeared to stimulate ideas and innovations. For example, one head teacher of a school for mentally handicapped children developed her own questionnaire for parents and visited each family at home in order to discuss their own views on ways in which parents and teachers could

work together more effectively and has since implemented several suggestions made by parents. Another
ran a series of evening discussions for teachers and
parents in all the City's special schools. In
addition, the University Centre for the In-service
Education of Teachers organised a series of evening
meetings on Partnership with Parents; these were
attended by teachers from a range of special schools
as well as a small number from ordinary schools. A
few parents also attended, some invited by teachers
in the schools attended by their child. Talks were
given by professionals from various disciplines and
by parents; evaluations at the end of the course indicated that several new initiatives in local
schools had arisen directly from suggestions made
during the course.

The Writing of Reports and Articles
A number of participants thought it would be useful
to write an article, either summarising the content
of the seminar or drawing out implications for
practice in their own country. As an example of the
seminar theme, it was also suggested that articles
could be written jointly by a parent and professional to appear in each others' journals; for
example, a joint article in a parents' journal or a
professional journal might have more impact than one
by either alone, even on the same theme. It was
noted that we would all benefit from changing our
reading and writing habits - 'we like to read what
we already know'.

In addition to articles which might be written
arising directly from the seminar, it would also be
useful to write articles illustrating examples of
collaboration between professionals and parents,
either in their own country or locality or elsewhere. It was felt that while there was much talk
about partnership, too little was known about actual
practice. It was also important to reflect the wide
variety of practice which had been illustrated in
the seminar and which had surprised some of its members. For example, it was useful to be reminded
that despite the general agreements that partnership
was a desirable goal, a different view was reflected
by the Dutch and Swedish participants of preferring
to leave teaching to teachers.

As a supplementary suggestion, it was also
pointed out that photographs, films and videotapes
illustrating parent-professional collaboration would
be a useful resource and could complement written
and spoken accounts of particular schemes.

225

Inviting Professionals to Parents' Meetings

Inviting professionals to parents' meetings was also commended. Parent groups could occasionally invite professionals to discuss aspects of their work at parents' meetings and to take part in discussion. For example, it was felt that some parents had incorrect or partially out-of-date views on the work of specific professional groups and perhaps tended to exaggerate their expertise and skills. Speech therapy was mentioned as a case in point: some parents still feel that speech therapists are qualified primarily to correct defects of articulation, whereas their role has greatly broadened during the past ten years. Not only are they concerned with all aspects of language and communication (including non-verbal methods such as signing and symbol systems), but also with pre-speech activities and even with methods of feeding children who cannot yet feed themselves and they are increasingly working through teachers and parents as intermediaries. In other words, they (like other specialists) are moving towards the model of a 'consultant' rather than exclusively as 'clinicians' working with individual children.

Similarly, it would be useful to be able to discuss ways in which the work of psychologists is moving away from individual intelligence testing towards the development of assessment of strengths and weaknesses and the designing of an individual programme for each child. Most important of all, parents would welcome opportunities to hear about developments in the education of mentally handicapped children – whether these concern content and curriculum or new methods of teaching.

Discussion also highlighted the importance of providing information about the range of services available to children at later stages of development; for example, the survey of families of mentally handicapped school leavers (Chapter 11) had shown that parents knew very little about the adult services to which their children were about to move or about ways in which these services had been developing in the recent past. In particular, few parents were aware of 'new thinking' on the provision of ordinary houses and on a wide range of alternatives for living, and most still assumed that the only alternative to living at home was a distant large institution (see Chapter 1).

Inviting Parents to Professionals' Meetings
Several participants also emphasised the value of
inviting parents to meetings of professionals. Very
few subjects were thought to be so technical or so
specialised as to be irrelevant to parents. In many
cases, it seemed, professionals organising seminars
and conferences had simply not thought of inviting
parents; it was not a question of deliberate exclusion. Parents themselves could suggest that it might
be helpful for invitations to be issued by writing
formally to organisers but sometimes the initiative
to invite parents came from a professional after a
friendly hint had been dropped by a parent. In the
U.K. the Association of Professions for the Mentally
Handicapped had been formed in 1973 with the express
purpose of bringing together in one organisation the
whole range of professional groups concerned with
mental handicap. After a few months, it was decided to include parents in the membership and they now
play a full and equal part both in national conferences and local meetings. Unfortunately, the title
of the Association still fails to reflect its membership.

Parents' Participation in Local and National Planning
Parents were increasingly being involved in membership of local planning or advisory committees and as
members of school boards. Parents are now legally
entitled to representation on school boards in some
countries (Norway and the U.K. were mentioned) and
are also playing an increasing part as members of
local committees planning the development of services for handicapped persons of all ages. Even so,
surveys have shown that this practice is still sometimes resisted. Participants felt that membership
of such key policy and planning bodies was essential; one national team decided that they would make
more determined attempts to secure parent representation on policy planning boards in their country.

Parents Contributing to the Training of Professionals
Several examples were given of ways in which parents
had contributed to the training of professionals and
further ways in which they might do so in the
future. Parent groups at local and national level
might make a formal approach to institutes of higher
education such as universities, polytechnics and
colleges, as well as to professional associations
involved in training, in order to enquire about the
extent to which the training of professionals includes some degree of awareness and preparation for

working with parents. It was generally agreed by
professionals that this subject had been barely
touched on either in their initial training or in
subsequent post-experience in-service courses,
despite the much greater degree of priority given to
the subject in current thinking.
    Although it was not feasible to think in terms
of specific training courses to equip professionals
with the skills needed to work with parents, few
people felt confident or competent in this relatively new area and it was thought that many would
welcome courses in which people would at least share
their experiences and problems as well as their
successes. Examples were quoted of courses for
doctors, teachers and social workers to which parents had contributed by discussing not only their
own personal experiences but also their ideas and
those of relevant parent groups and organisations on
ways in which professionals could develop better
working relationships with parents. Parents are
sometimes in a better position to draw attention to
examples of good practice in different parts of the
country; their journals and special contacts provide relevant information of which professionals may
not necessarily be aware. One teacher who was in a
good position to influence his local teacher training curriculum proposed to draft a chapter on co-
operation between parents and professionals for the
consideration of the appropriate committee.

Joint Training of Parents and Professionals
Rapid development of new methods of teaching and
working with mentally handicapped people makes it
essential to provide short practical courses on
specific topics. Unfortunately, many of these
courses tend to be organised for one group of professionals, either by universities or by single
professional associations - e.g. those concerned
with the further training of doctors, teachers,
psychologists, social workers, therapists, etc. It
is increasingly recognised that much of this training could be given to multidisciplinary groups,
since few of these new developments are so specific
that they are relevant to only one profession.
Similarly, there is no reason why opportunities to
participate in such courses should not be thrown
open to parents. It may well be that only a small
number of parents would be interested or willing to
attend but it is possible that many more would do so
if direct encouragement was provided for them to do
so. This might be done by specific invitations to

the local parent organisations or by schools and other agencies ensuring that parents are informed about available courses. Ideally, however, a personal invitation by a professional to one or more parents is likely to help parents to feel 'comfortable' in attending meetings and courses where they are likely to be outnumbered by professionals and where some of the discussions may at first seem remote and technical. Parents may feel diffident about attending such meetings but it helps if they know other parents will attend or contribute as speakers.

University Extra-Mural Departments or Adult Education Colleges have an important role in the development of multidisciplinary courses which make a deliberate effort to include parents. Such colleges are 'neutral' ground - i.e. they are not obviously associated with a particular profession or discipline and they provide opportunities for the public at large to take courses in any subject of their choice (Mittler, 1979).

The University of Manchester's Department of Extra-Mural Studies has been organising such courses over a number of years in different parts of Greater Manchester covering ten local government districts. These courses are often held in a school but make every effort to recruit both parents and professionals from the whole district and not just those from the school where the course is based. The content of the courses includes a substantial practical element in which participants practise various teaching techniques, sometimes using 'role play' in which one person pretends to be a handicapped child with a specific learning difficulty while others act the role of 'teacher'. Use is also made of specially prepared video-recordings illustrating particular teaching and rehabilitative methods as examples of good practice. Participants are introduced to methods of assessment and recording, such as the use of developmental checklists, and ways in which these can be used to design an individual programme. Quite apart from the skill-based elements, such courses can also provide opportunities for a free discussion on wider-ranging topics. The important point is that parents and professionals attend as equals, not because one group has made a special effort to 'involve' or 'invite' the other.

PARENTS AS EMPLOYERS

The seminar reminded us that in a number of countries it is parents who employ professionals and who

determine how a service shall be run. This is the
case in countries where voluntary societies are
themselves the main providers of a service, and are
grant-aided for the purpose by government or from
public money - for example, in the Netherlands, in
Belgium, in New Zealand, in some of the Australian
states, and in several other countries. This is an
unusual situation for professionals in Britain where
the voluntary sector provides very few major services itself, but rather works as a pressure group to
increase the quality and quantity of public services.

     Where parents are employers and policy makers,
the quality of the parent-professional partnership
assumes a somewhat different dimension. What
happens, for example, when the original generation
of 'pioneering parents' is succeeded by a new generation of parents with very different ideas on
priorities - for example concerning ordinary housing
and integrated education, in contrast to 'village
communities' and special schools? (See Roseneau and
Provencal (1981) for a sensitive discussion of parental misgivings about community services).

     These questions are reflected in a recent com-
parative study of mental handicap services in a
number of different countries prepared by Heron and
Myers (1983) who contrast a variety of models of
service delivery - e.g. in large federal countries
such as U.S.A., Canada, Australia with smaller non-
federal countries such as New Zealand, Israel, the
Netherlands, Denmark, Sweden and the U.K. Their
account reflects rapidly changing philosophies
among the voluntary societies. Moreover, it describes increasingly complex relationships with
governments who provide funds but who are not necessarily in sympathy with the policies of the voluntary societies - which may be too conservative or
too radical for them.

PARENTS AS MONITORS OF THE QUALITY OF SERVICES

Parent movements are also beginning to play an increasing part in monitoring the quality of services
provided by professionals, and insisting that professionals should express a greater degree of
accountability. Parent groups have issued their
own 'standards documents', such as MENCAP's (1977)
Stamina documents (concerned with minimum standards
in schools, adult training centres and residential
services) and have also been trained to use existing
methods of evaluating the quality of services. Many

parent groups in North America have become proficient in the use of the 'Program Analysis of Service Systems' (PASS lll) (Wolfensberger and Glenn, 1975), a rigorous system of evaluation based on principles of normalisation. PASS is also now beginning to be used in Britain as one of a number of approaches to monitoring the quality of services. In parts of Canada, parents are encouraged by professionals themselves to monitor the quality of the programme being provided and to express both their satisfaction and dissatisfaction (Brynelsen, Gall and Sax, 1982).

PARTICIPATION AND DECISION MAKING BY MENTALLY HANDI-CAPPED PEOPLE

One further topic was thought to be of particular importance and merited extensive discussion. This concerned ways of helping mentally handicapped people themselves to express a much greater degree of choice, to have more opportunities to participate in decisions concerning the quality of services being provided for them and in plans concerning ways in which their needs were to be met in the future.

Brief references were made during the seminar to a number of developments in both practice and research which were potentially of great significance and which might prove as important and innovative in the 1980's as 'parental involvement' had been in some countries in the 1970s.

The Development and Rapid Growth in Some Countries of Self-Advocacy Movements

The most far-reaching of these was undoubtedly the American 'People First' movement which demonstrated beyond doubt that mentally handicapped people were able to speak forcefully about their situation and their needs, and to articulate their needs both among themselves and before parents and professionals (Williams and Shoultz, 1982). The People First Movement has now become a major organisation, with annual national and regional conferences, with teams of speakers who meet local policy makers and decision makers and who also attend professional conferences and present their point of view.

Groups of mentally handicapped people both from People First and from comparable organisations in other countries attended the 1982 World Congress of the International League of Societies for Persons with Mental Handicap in Nairobi where they had the choice of participating in main sessions as well as

231

organising sessions for themselves. A delegation of three mentally handicapped people has also addressed a meeting of the General Assembly of the United Nations organisation in order to make a plea for a greater degree of recognition of the needs of mentally handicapped people.

No Bar to Participation
These developments are by no means restricted to the most able mentally handicapped people - i.e. those who are in the 'mild' or 'educable' ranges of ability. The self-advocacy movement makes every effort to ensure that less able and more severely impaired people are encouraged to participate, often despite severe physical and communication handicaps. The film 'People First' made in the early period of the movement illustrated how moderately and severely handicapped people could participate in meetings and discussions in a variety of ways, not necessarily by addressing a meeting, and appeared able to follow the main points of a discussion and to express choice in decision making.

Student Committees
A survey of Adult Training Centres by a HARC doctoral student, Bronach Crawley (1982) has established that well over a quarter of Adult Training Centres now have a 'student committee', with some form of active participation and representation by mentally handicapped people attending the Centres. One Centre (Avro Centre, Southend) secured affiliation of the Centre and its students to the National Union of Students, thus potentially gaining the status and concessionary privileges available to all other registered students in the U.K.

Communicating Opinions
A number of research workers in HARC and elsewhere are developing and evaluating a range of instruments designed to help mentally handicapped people to express preference in a number of key areas - e.g. choice of preferred job (*Illustrated Vocational Inventory*, Whelan and Reiter, 1980; *Me at Work*, Whelan and Speake, 1980); choice of leisure activities (*Junior Interest Profile*, Jeffree and Cheseldine, 1982); and evaluation of the quality of the residential environment (Howie, Cuming and Raynes, 1982). Howie also reviews a range of other client-centred instruments developed in various centres in Europe and North America, as well as her own innovative studies in New Zealand.

232

PARENTS, PROFESSIONALS AND MENTALLY HANDICAPPED
PEOPLE

The rapid growth of self-advocacy in the last few
years is not only of great interest in its own
right. It also raises a number of important issues
in relation both to the parent movement itself and
to parent-professional partnership. What if the
views of a mentally handicapped person are in conflict with those of the parents? If the views of
professionals are in sympathy with those of the
young person, whose rights are paramount - those of
the parents who are still responsible for the 'care'
of their son or daughter, the 'experts' who are paid
to promote their interests and protect their rights,
or the mentally handicapped people themselves, with
their own rights and responsibilities as adult
citizens? What about the adult in residential care
whose parents still want a voice in the programme?
And what happens when a mentally handicapped person
expresses a point of view which is consistent with
the wishes of neither the parents nor the professionals?

    Conventional wisdom as well as established
practice tend to suggest that mentally handicapped
people, almost by definition, are unlikely to 'know
their own minds', are 'easily swayed by their peers'
or by 'what they have just seen on the television',
and that they are 'unrealistic'. On the other hand,
research findings consistently suggest that staff
and parents frequently and massively under-estimate
the abilities even of mentally handicapped people
whom they know well. Indeed, it has been suggested
that under-estimation of their abilities constitutes
their most significant handicap, since it prevents
staff from exposing them to the challenge of demand
and opportunity to learn on the grounds that they
are 'unlikely to be able to benefit'.

    Perhaps the self-advocacy movement provides the
most telling illustration of this theme, since many
people still do not accept that mentally handicapped
people should or can express a point of view about
their own situation, or participate 'meaningfully'
in decision making, even in areas which immediately
affect their day-to-day lives. Similar doubts were
at one time expressed about disabled people generally, though the 'consumerism' movement is now very
strong amongst physically disabled adults, who constitute an extremely powerful and articulate lobby
both at national and international levels, and whose
advocacy sometimes takes the form of militant anti-

professionalism.

These issues are at the forefront of discussion at the beginning of the 1980s and are likely to remain prominent for many years to come. We are only now beginning to confront the adult status of mentally handicapped people and are at the threshold of considering how they can be helped to express choice and decision making in issues that deeply affect their lives. This will remain one of the most challenging tasks for partnership not only between parents and professionals but for both of them with mentally handicapped people themselves.

REFERENCES

Blunden, R. and Revill, S. (1980) A behavioural approach. In The Handicapped Person in the Community (Unit 5, Block 2). Milton Keynes: Open University Press

Brynelsen, D., Gall, R., and Sax, P. (1982) Parent-Professional Partnership Profile. Toronto: National Institute on Mental Retardation (in preparation)

Crawley, B. (1982) Self-advocacy in Britain. Paper presented to the 6th World Congress, International Association for the Scientific Study of Mental Deficiency, Toronto, Canada, August 25th, 1982

Georgiades, N. and Phillimore, M. (1975) The myth of the hero-innovator and alternative strategies for organisational change. In C.C. Kiernan and F.P. Woodford (eds.) Behaviour Modification with the Severely Retarded. Amsterdam: Associated Scientific Publishers

Heron, A. and Myers, M. (1983) Intellectual Impairment: the Battle against Handicap. New York and London: Academic Press (in press)

Houts, P.S. and Scott, R. (1975) Goal Planning with Developmentally Disabled Persons. Hershey Medical Centre: Pennsylvania State University

Howie, D., Cuming, J. and Raynes, N. (1982) Development of tools to facilitate participation by retarded persons in residential evaluation procedures. (in preparation)

Jeffree, D. and Cheseldine, S. (1982) Junior Interest Profile. Manchester: Hester Adrian Research Centre

Mittler, P. (1979) People not Patients: Problems and Policies in Mental Handicap. London: Methuen

Mittler, P. and Beasley, D. (1982) A Multi-National

Family Training Workshop. Report to UNESCO and UN. Brussels: International League of Societies for Persons with Mental Handicap

Rosenau, N. and Provencal, G. (1981) Community placement and parental misgivings. *Mental Retardation*, 31, 3-11

Royal Society for Mentally Handicapped Children and Adults (1977) *Minimum Standards for Local Services*. London: MENCAP

Whelan, E. and Reiter, S. (1980) *Illustrated Vocational Inventory*. Manchester: Copewell Publications (HARC)

Whelan, E. and Speake, B. (1980) *Me at Work*. Manchester: Copewell Publications (HARC)

Williams, P. and Shoultz, B. (1982) *We Can Speak for Ourselves: Self-Advocacy by Mentally Handicapped People*. London: Souvenir Press

Wolfensberger, W. and Glenn, L. (1975) *Program Analysis of Service Systems* (PASS 3) Toronto (York University): National Institute on Mental Retardation

NOTES ON CONTRIBUTORS

Sally Beveridge

Director, Anson House Preschool Project, Hester
Adrian Research Centre, Manchester University

Dana Brynelsen

Provincial Advisor, Infant Development Programs,
Vancouver, British Columbia, Canada

Sally Cheseldine

Research Fellow, Parents and Their Handicapped
Teenagers Project, Hester Adrian Research Centre,
Manchester University

Cliff Cunningham

Director, Infant Project, Hester Adrian Research
Centre, Manchester University

Pauline Fairbrother

Vice-chairperson, Royal Society for Mentally Handicapped Children and Adults, London

Jill Gardner

Educational Psychologist, Education Department
Psychological Services, Walsall

Dorothy Jeffree

Director, Parents and their Handicapped Teenagers Project, Hester Adrian Research Centre, Manchester University

Helen McConachie

Honorary Research Fellow, Hester Adrian Research Centre, Manchester University

Helle Mittler

Senior Social Worker, School Psychological and Child Guidance Service, Manchester

Peter Mittler

Professor of Special Education, and Director, Hester Adrian Research Centre, Manchester University

Shirley Rheubottom

Honorary Research Fellow, Hester Adrian Research Centre, Manchester University

James Ross

Director of Welfare Services, Royal Society for Mentally Handicapped Children and Adults, London

Philippa Russell

Senior Officer, Voluntary Council for Handicapped Children, National Children's Bureau, London

LIST OF OTHER SEMINAR PARTICIPANTS

Austria

Megan Hayward, physiotherapist
Sigrun Scheirl, parent

238

Belgium

Lucienne van Loon, parent
Claudine van Malderen, teacher

Denmark

Jørgen Kristensen, teacher
Gugu Kristoffersen, parent

France

Henri Bissonnier, professor of special education
Yvonne de Laval, parent

Great Britain

John Chillag, parent
Rita Flanagan, social worker

Netherlands

Enno Felix, Bishop Bekkers Institute
Mariet van Hattum, parent
Ms L Klaus, observer
Sandor Németh, Bishop Bekkers Institute
Marian Verhaart-van Zijderveld, observer
Bob van Zijderveld, social worker

Norway

Berit Røhmen, parent
Kari Storemyr, teacher

Sweden

Erica Lund, parent
Henrik Pelling, psychiatrist

West Germany

Sonja Barthel, teacher
Renate Börner, parent
Christoph Hublow, teacher

INDEX